The Makings
of a
Philanthropic
Fundraiser

Ronald Alan Knott

Foreword by Patricia F. Lewis
Prologue by Milton Murray

The Makings
of a
Philanthropic
Fundraiser

*The Instructive Example
of Milton Murray*

Jossey-Bass Publishers · San Francisco

For sales outside the United States contact Maxwell Macmillan International Publishing Group, 866 Third Avenue, New York, New York 10022

Printed on acid-free paper and manufactured in the United States of America

The paper used in this book meets the State of California requirements for recycled paper (50 percent recycled waste, including 10 percent post-consumer waste), which are the strictest guidelines for recycled paper currently in use in the United States.

Library of Congress Cataloging-in-Publication Data

Knott, Ron.
    The makings of a philanthropic fundraiser : the instructive example of Milton Murray / Ronald Alan Knott ; foreword by Patricia F. Lewis.
      p.   cm. — (The Jossey-Bass nonprofit sector series)
    Includes bibliographical references and index.
    ISBN 1-55542-424-4
    1. Fundraising—United States.   2. Murray, Milton J.   3. Fund-raisers (Persons)—United States—Biography.   4. Charities—United States.   I. Title II. Series.
HV41.9.U5R58   1992
361.7—dc20
[B]   91-35842
                                              CIP

FIRST EDITION
HB Printing   10 9 8 7 6 5 4 3 2 1   *Code 9220*

The Jossey-Bass
Nonprofit Sector Series

Contents

Foreword

Some learn by doing. Some learn by reading. Some learn by example. This book, which reads like an extended conversation with Milton Murray, offers all three types of learning experiences.

If one is looking for a book that explains the step-by-step techniques of fundraising, this is not the book to read. However, if the reader would like to explore process and motivation, *The Makings of a Philanthropic Fundraiser* will be of great value. It provides that adjunct experience so needed in striving toward the next level of professionalism. While we all need to know the "how to's," are we not better practitioners if we also know the "what for's"?

Milt Murray has been honored by almost every organization involved in philanthropy. He is by nature enthusiastic about people and their abilities, totally dedicated to the basic principles of philanthropic fundraising, and persistent beyond the imagination of most of us. He is curious about what others are thinking and doing. He shares his own thoughts and activities when asked (he is not boastful and hence shies away from proffering too much about himself). He is a teacher by his very actions.

It is this last attribute that the book capitalizes upon. *The Makings of a Philanthropic Fundraiser* explores Milt's life, his activities, his dreams, his successful and unsuccessful attempts and plans. By the way, Milt never views unsuccessful experiences as failures but rather as opportunities for greater persistence. The examples of such experiences offered in this book are wonderful lessons in how to turn lemons into lemonade.

When I first met Milt sometime in the late seventies, our conversation turned to the need for materials on fundraising for non–English-speaking people. Together we lamented the lack of translations of some good basic books such as Seymour's *Designs for Fund Raising.* As I was about to move on to a meeting, Milt called me back and said, "You know, I've gotten them to translate Seymour's book into Spanish." It seems he had been using it for some time in his fundraising throughout South America. With his usual generosity, he offered to send me a copy of this little jewel, which has since traveled on loan to others. Milt, pioneering where others would like to be!

I, and countless others, have received Milt's postcards from Brazil and his phone calls from airports. By example, he provides wonderful lessons in communication, gentle persuasion, . . . and recognition. For years I have been learning from him.

Milt Murray is the ultimate example of one who lives and breathes his commitment to his profession. As such, he has been a role model for many in this emerging and highly desirable profession of philanthropic fundraising. Notice the qualifying adjective *philanthropic,* for you will see it often as you read the book. It is Milton's descriptor. His persistence in its use is working. I am seeing it more frequently in written materials, and I find myself using the term much more as time goes by.

Formalized philanthropic fundraising is maturing as a profession. On reaching full maturity, the field needs literature—documentation and research. Books such as this, focused on the motivations of a highly regarded early practitioner, bring substance, understanding, and perspective. Technical expertise and guidelines are woven into it throughout.

Who should read this book? I suggest that it will be valuable for beginning as well as more experienced professional philanthropic fundraisers. And I think it could add to the understanding of the fundraising process for those who work with philanthropic fundraisers, either as not-for-profit executives or as volunteers.

The reader will learn much: the importance of commitment to one's own values and the glory of optimistic persistence (or is it persistent optimism?). These are the keys to Milt's successes and the lessons for us all, carefully explored and taught in these examples from Milton Murray's career.

December 1991   Patricia F. Lewis
President and Chief Executive Officer
National Society of Fund Raising Executives

Preface

Few books in the rapidly expanding body of fundraising literature attempt to put flesh on the skeleton of theory and practice. This book, through an examination of the career of Milton Murray, makes that attempt.

It is intended as real-life affirmation and inspiration for practicing and future philanthropic fundraisers. At the same time, many of the principles articulated here are relevant and applicable to men and women who long for success in any line of work. Although the book is an informal presentation, not a professional biography, it gives clear insights into the attributes that have earned Murray the highest respect and honor among his colleagues. Heavily anecdotal in approach, *The Makings of a Philanthropic Fundraiser* is a readable and informative demonstration and explication of a few of the qualities and characteristics of one great professional who has made an indelible impression on the organization to which he has committed his life, and on the profession that has been his passion for forty-two years.

Jerold Panas, in his book *Born to Raise* (1988), has artfully described or listed some of the individual characteristics of high achievement evident in the careers of ten of the nation's great philanthropic fundraisers, among whom Panas includes Milton Murray. The present book expands on that information, demonstrating how nine important characteristics or assets have figured in Murray's life and helped him achieve greatness.

The characteristics are his remarkable *energy* and ability to efficiently accomplish great amounts of work; his search for and sense of professional *calling*, instilled during his young adult years as a college student and as a soldier during World War II; his *leadership* in establishing new ideas and ways of doing things within his own employment context and the larger professional community; his *mentoring* of young people in the profession, and his admiration for the philanthropic possibilities of the next generation; his *creativity* in solving problems and achieving goals; his *persistence* in finishing a task, no matter how difficult; his delight in *anonymity;* his *loyalty and commitment* to his organization and profession; and his *common touch*—the consummate ability to make the profession he loves relevant to the layperson.

The reader will find a chapter devoted to each of these assets or characteristics. Each chapter contains examples from Murray's own experience, supplemented by his vast knowledge of others' professional experience, and provides a forum for Murray to interpret that experience for general application. The primary body of research for this book is contained in a long series of taped interviews with Murray and his colleagues. Extensive quotations from those interviews are used liberally throughout the book.

In fairness, it must be noted that this is an intentionally admiring assessment of Murray, though its sponsors are convinced that even the most earnest attempt at dead objectivity would yield pretty much the same result.

Even though this is not "Milton Murray's Story," it clearly is a view of the man as he is grudgingly willing to let himself be known. Had matters been left entirely up to him, the book would never have been written. Self-promotion is not his style. Excessive exposure could, he complains, undercut his effectiveness in the great work to which he has devoted himself. The book came about because many of Murray's admirers—professional colleagues, philanthropists, and friends—politely but persistently ignored his protests.

One of those Murray admirers and colleagues is Deborah Pontynen Case, of Maranatha Volunteers International, in Sacramento, California. Her vision, persistence, and fundraising skills made the book a reality. Her sometimes exaggerated claims about my abilities as an author won me the golden opportunity to write this book under the sponsorship of the Milton Murray Foundation for Philanthropy, and her constant encouragement along the way made this project one of the most enjoyable jobs I have ever had. Don Noble, also of the Maranatha organization, made many of the key contacts with the donors who generously underwrote this project.

As I have noted, this book was sponsored by the Milton Murray Foundation for Philanthropy. The small foundation, with assets in 1991 of more than $260,000, honors the accomplishments of Milton Murray by promoting increased awareness and understanding of philanthropy in American society and by assisting in the professional growth of development officers and staff of charitable institutions. Since its establishment in 1987, the foundation has been directed by a board of trustees chaired by Henry A. Rosso. I am grateful to the foundation for the credibility its sponsorship has added to this enterprise.

There are others whose contribution I must acknowledge. Brandon Breckenridge, during a busy year as president of his high school graduating class at Takoma Academy in Takoma Park, Maryland, diligently and accurately transcribed scores of hours of taped interviews. I must also thank the many Murray associates who freely gave their time to be interviewed in person or by telephone. Special research assistance was willingly supplied by Louise Dederen and James Ford, curators of the Adventist Heritage Center at Andrews University; Bert B. Haloviak of the Office of Archives and Statistics at Seventh-day Adventist Church Headquarters in Silver Spring, Maryland; and James Nix, chair of the Department of Archives and Special Collections at Loma Linda University in California.

Several people gave invaluable help by reading portions of the manuscript as it developed. Among those I must thank are B. Lyn Behrens, David Harris, Roland Hegstad, Lisa Marks, Sheree Parris Nudd, Russell Raker, Neal C. Wilson, and Milton Murray's staff at Adventist World Headquarters. Of all the readers of the manuscript, however, none read it with more care and concern for its success than my editors, Alan Shrader and Susan Abel of Jossey-Bass, whose style of guidance during revisions should be the dream of every author.

And then there is Milton Murray himself, who in the truest sense made this book possible.

Last, I must thank my wife, Esther. Her encouragement and support of my work on this project, and her perfect love during this our first year and a half of marriage, enabled me never for a moment to forget that I was married to her, and not to this book.

Silver Spring, Maryland   Ronald Alan Knott
December 1991

Prologue

As one who has thriven on anonymity, avoided center stage, and enjoyed seeing the chiefs and others spotlighted, the ultimate paradox is the publication of a book about myself. How can it be?

The first suggestion for a book came in the late seventies from Kathleen Butler of Overland Park, Kansas, who urged me to record my personal and professional experiences—even sending me a how-to book on writing an autobiography. I appreciated her friendship and was flattered by the idea, but I knew that such a volume was not for me to write. And even if it were, who would read it?

In 1982 I was lecturing at Pacific Union College, calling attention to the virtues of philanthropy as a career. In that class of twenty-five students, a young woman, Deborah Pontynen Case, decided that my observations should be published. However, it was not until the late eighties that she confronted me with the urgent need for a book. I had no trouble reminding her that I had plenty of work, didn't need another chore, and, even if time weren't an issue, saw no point in writing a book about myself. Furthermore, I would not feel comfortable putting such a volume together. It did not make sense for me to change my lifelong habit of making others look good and helping institutions to be more successful, in order to draw attention to any good I may have been a party to.

But Deborah is a persistent sort of person. She was farsighted where I was myopic. We met for dinner on the West Coast, and she came up with the question, "Will you cooperate and help in putting together a book if we engage a writer?" I told her I'd think about it and get back to her. As I confronted the realization that this woman was serious, I reflected on the matter and conceded that she might have a point. It could be that a description of characteristics and qualities in my makeup as seen by others could be of some interest and possible value. Having been challenged throughout my life by CEOs, faculty members, medical staff members, friends, and even my family to understand the what, why, and how of philanthropy, I began to think that an attempt to inform and interpret might be justified. Cooperation on my part in producing a book might assist others to understand the validity and importance of the work, and perhaps a book would add respectability to the profession in a way that my person could not.

So, partly to placate Deborah and partly because I began to see the possibilities, I agreed to the book on two conditions: first, that it would be a means of attracting young people to the career, and second, that although there are many motives for giving, the book must reflect my conviction that philanthropy is ultimately based on deep moral and spiritual values, which bring satisfaction and joy to both donors and recipients.

I trust that this book will help leaders to better understand those of us who staff philanthropic endeavors, and I hope that it will help administrators to respect development officers as peers and colleagues, even though they are not always in the limelight. I also hope that it will inspire young men and women to realize the numerous satisfactions that come to those who work behind the scenes but are vital to the process of charitable giving in this country.

My ultimate dream would be fulfilled if CEOs, donors, trustees, and development staffs, using the whole spectrum of human and financial resources, talents, and skills, could see themselves as collaborators in helping people become the better for having given to others. I think that *The Makings of a Philanthropic Fundraiser* suggests an interdependence of all these human elements in making philanthropy successful and inspiring.

The oft-quoted "No man is an island" has special significance for those of us who work in philanthropy. At the risk of neglecting a name or two, I submit that the following men and women significantly influenced my professionalism and thus are, in good measure, responsible for the contents of this book. They are the people who made a difference to me. I list their names in my private hall of fame, with the hope that the reader will recognize opportunities to help managers, peers, and beginners along the way and thereby become a more effective "servant-leader." My listing, more or less in the order in which these people influenced me and my work, is as follows:

- Walter P. Elliott: The chairman of the board of the College of Medical Evangelists (now Loma Linda University) who kept assuring me in the 1950s that what I was doing was important and that I should pay little heed to other leaders who questioned the validity of my work. Although he was three decades older and six rungs above me professionally, he reached down to encourage me from time to time.
- Ada Turner: The only person I know of who at a glance could distinguish between 10- and 12-point periods in type! From her I learned the importance of detail and that every job must excel. But even more importantly, I learned that a professional must follow his or her convictions.
- Dan Benefiel: The professional who skillfully shoehorned me from public relations into philanthropy at an important juncture in my career.

- Luis Garibay Gutiérrez and Alfonso Marín Jiménez: Mexican university executives who accelerated my professional conversion—and thus my effectiveness—from the Anglo-Saxon to the Latin culture. They also live lives that have inspired me by demonstrating a special commitment to their society.
- Neal C. Wilson: The church leader who, with his vision of the future in philanthropy for Adventist health and education systems during the last twenty-five years, ran interference to overcome traditional resistance to new approaches. His confidence in me was sobering and compelling.
- Martha Sterner: A competent secretary and office manager who kept the office functioning during a vital six-year period when I was there only one or two working days per month. Her superior loyalty and devotion helped to make a difference.
- Thomas and Violet Zapara: A committed Christian couple who time and time again recognized opportunities to inspire thousands of others to contribute to important causes and thereby boldly initiated and established programs that supported people and institutions through philanthropy. Their vision matched their resources.
- David Colwell, Sheree Parris Nudd, and LuAnn Wolfe: These able young professionals, through their creativity and hard work, kept assuring me that an investment in the next generation was justified. Their energy and initiative helped to make it happen.

The professional networking provided by the Council for the Advancement and Support of Education, the National Association for Hospital Development (now the Association for Healthcare Philanthropy), and the National Society of Fund Raising Executives has been incredibly important to me throughout my career. Their conferences, their leaders, their national staffs, and their publications have helped me to grow, to explore frontiers, and to get things done; most of all, they inspired me to do what I can as a member for the whole. I pay special tribute to the commitment these and similar organizations have to philanthropy. Other entities where my input has been negligible, although I have benefited from their presence, are such organizations as INDEPENDENT SECTOR, the Association of Governing Boards, the American Association of Fund-Raising Counsel and its trust, and the National Center for Nonprofit Boards.

My thanks go to a thoughtful and considerate staff who, already overextended, assisted in every way in the preparation of the manuscript for this book. Of course, I pay special tribute to Ronald Knott, who worked over a span of eighteen months to research, write, and rewrite the manuscript. The book is ample demonstration of his competence, for which I am grateful. What the reader should also know is that he adjusted to some of my unearthly working schedules to get the job done.

But outranking all these colleagues is my friend and companion, Virginia. She has been a patient and unassuming wife who for more than four decades has stood by my side. Her management of our own limited resources has kept me from giving it all away! The professional life I have lived would not have been possible without her understanding. Our children, Keith and Deanne, have also given up some of their dad so that others could be helped. This trio deserves a special expression of gratitude for still accepting me in the family. They have given more than most will ever realize, and I am particularly grateful to them for allowing me to enjoy such a wonderful career.

I still believe that anonymity contributes to our professional success. However, if by giving it up I can help my colleagues of the future to be better understood by CEOs, donors, and trustees, the sacrifice will have been well worth it. Time will tell.

Silver Spring, Maryland   Milton Murray
December 1991

The Author

Ronald Alan Knott is an editorial consultant for the Adventist Development and Relief Agency International (ADRA) in Silver Spring, Maryland. He received his B.A. degree (1981) in English and religion from Atlantic Union College in South Lancaster, Massachusetts.

From 1981 to 1990, Knott worked in higher education advancement, most recently as director of public relations at Andrews University in Berrien Springs, Michigan.

The Makings
of a
Philanthropic
Fundraiser

1

Who Is
Milton Murray?

So long as we love we serve.
                    —*Robert Louis Stevenson,*
                    Lay Morals

At 9:00 P.M. on February 27, 1991, George Bush made a nation-ally televised speech to the American people from his desk in the Oval Office at the White House. He announced a tentative end to hostilities in the short and one-sided Persian Gulf War. Milton Murray missed the live broadcast of the president's announcement. He was working late at the office, getting ready for a trip from his home in Beltsville, Maryland, to San Antonio, Texas, for the annual meeting of the National Society of Fund-Raising Executives (NSFRE), where he would receive the society's highest professional honor.

By 5:30 the next morning Murray had finished packing his personal belongings for the trip. With a few minutes left before the company driver would take him and his wife from their modest home in Beltsville to the airport for an early flight to San Antonio, he switched on the TV and caught a rebroadcast of President Bush's speech. Like millions of other Americans, Murray delighted in what he heard the president say. Unlike those millions of others, Murray also delighted in what he saw on the president's desk.

Within reach of the president's left hand as he delivered his historic address was a result of one of Milton Murray's recent professional brainstorms. A copy of the 1991 "Giving Is Caring" page-a-day calendar rested in a display stand hand-crafted from exotic curly koa wood by one of Murray's donor friends. The annual calendar contains 365 uplifting thoughts promoting the philanthropic impulse. Murray had collected great quotations about caring and service for many years, and in 1986 he began publishing a calendar. In six years he saw more than 250,000 copies reach the hands of business leaders, politicians, and philanthropists, large and small, throughout American society. President Bush had accepted his special-edition copy the previous December from Robert Folkenberg, the president of the Seventh-day Adventist Church and Murray's boss.

George Bush's speech marked a moment of immense relief and triumph for the American people. It also marked a moment of intense personal satisfaction for Milton Murray, for whom the moment took on mythic meaning. It confirmed his professional convictions. His methods worked.

Five days later, Murray made a speech of his own. For a man whose in-house professional renown largely rests, at least to the casual observer, on his penchant for publishing the profound and pithy comments of others, his acceptance speech was remarkably spare. The two thousand members of the NSFRE who jammed the San Antonio Convention Center's great hall might have braced themselves for something different. The entire speech, in which he accepted the Outstanding Fund-Raising Executive of the Year Award, was a mere 750 words long and contained only two brief quotations from others. The first quotation Murray took from a Paul Goodman novel: "If there is no community for you, young man, young woman, make it yourself." The second was an aphorism commonly attributed to Churchill: "We make a living by what we get. We make a life by what we give."

Murray's use of these two simple thoughts, in the context of his short speech, was primarily homiletic, to make specific points. Examined together, outside of his speech, they profoundly make the measure of the man, perhaps better than any other combination of two wise sayings could. The Goodman quote richly summarizes Murray's lifelong practice and preaching of the pioneering spirit. The Churchill comment describes a life—in Murray's case, a pioneering life—utterly devoted to philanthropic endeavor. Melded into one, these two ideas describe the essence of who Milton Murray is: a pioneer for philanthropy.

That pioneering spirit counted much toward winning Murray the NSFRE award. During four decades he has established several public relations and development programs, has consulted for more than fifty institutions in twelve countries, has directly led campaigns that have raised more than $60 million, and has been a founder of, or primary agitator for, programs that have raised $250 million more. He brought about *Campañas Para Obtención de Fondos* (1970), the Spanish translation of Harold J. Seymour's *Designs for Fund-Raising* (1966; 2nd ed. 1988) and organized the first conference in Spanish for development professionals in Latin American universities sponsored by the Council for Advancement and Support of Education (CASE).

Murray's publications, including topical "how-to" booklets and collections of quotations and fundraising humor, have made an important contribution to the practice and profile of philanthropy in American life. Sales for the "Giving Is Caring" calendar increase every year.

Murray is a member of CASE, a certified member of NSFRE, an accredited member of the Public Relations Society of America (PRSA), and a Fellow of the Association for Healthcare Philanthropy (AHP), formerly the National Association for Hospital Development. He is a member of the

National Philanthropy Day Committee (NPD) and chairman of the NPD subcommittees on finance and on the establishment of a postal issue on philanthropy. First elected a trustee of Henry Rosso's Fund Raising School in 1976, Murray served as chairman from 1986 until the school was absorbed into Indiana University–Purdue University at Indianapolis as part of the Center on Philanthropy. He chaired the AHP Educational Fund from 1982 to 1986 and the NSFRE annual Every Member campaign in 1988–90.

In 1980, Murray received the Harold J. Seymour Award, the highest honor bestowed by the AHP. He received an honorary doctor of laws degree from Andrews University in 1985. In 1990 he was named outstanding fundraiser by both the Detroit, Michigan, and Washington, D.C., chapters of NSFRE, whose nominations initiated the national award at the San Antonio convention in March 1991.

In explaining or accounting for these accomplishments, Murray looks to his past and to his upbringing. For, perhaps as much as any man, Milton Murray is a product of his heritage. That heritage is enormously instructive about the man himself and informs his personal and professional philosophy. A few summary points must be understood for context. Murray himself can make them best.

> I came from a background where conservative Protestantism played a very large role in family life. My grandmother, widowed in her early thirties when her farmer husband was killed by the kick of a horse, raised my father, Walter Murray, as a Seventh-day Adventist. My father grew up extremely poor, but determined nonetheless to get a secondary and college education in Adventist schools. It was a long, hard grind with school wedged in around the edges of massive amounts of student labor. But on May 19, 1919, at age twenty-five, he graduated from Emmanuel Missionary College, now Andrews University, in Berrien Springs, Michigan. He was president of the graduating class.

Later the same day he married Golda James in the college chapel. My mother had grown up in less arduous circumstances. Her father held a Ph.D. degree in languages from the University of Munich and had taught at Wesleyan University in Connecticut, Miami University in Ohio, and Albert G. Lane Technical High School in Chicago. Unlike my father, my mother grew up as a middle-class Adventist in relatively sophisticated university towns or in the throb of a new American metropolis.

However different their backgrounds may have been, my parents had the same views about Christian service. During their engagement they accepted a "call" from the Adventist World Headquarters to go to South America as missionaries immediately upon their graduation and marriage.

So I was raised in a missionary home in Brazil, Peru, and Argentina, where my father held a series of increasingly responsible positions in church administration. My father's work was the focus of family life, and I absorbed a deep understanding of, and commitment to, the church organization he worked for.

My two sisters and I were taught to live simply and to care for others. Adventists are encouraged to return 10 percent of their income to the church as biblically mandated tithe and to make substantial contributions in addition to tithe to help other worthy church endeavors. We were taught this practice from our childhood.

My parents believed that we should be educated in Christian schools. They went without many amenities normally enjoyed by the families of executives of my father's rank so that we could attend church-operated schools.

When I was fourteen, my parents sent me off to the one church-operated secondary school in Argentina, about two hundred miles from my home. The expense of keeping me in a private school put heavy pressure on the family budget. I didn't get any break on tuition, even though my father was chairman of the school board. Once I wrote home asking for money, and my dad wrote back the following:

> You mention something about needing some money. Really, we are awful short for this right now. We are sacrificing here at home almost beyond what we should but it seems necessary in order to keep your school bill paid. The girls are not studying music. We are eating sweet potatoes until the price of Irish potatoes comes down. Have cut butter lately quite largely, just in order to keep our accounts where they should be. You see, we have to pay 52.50 [Argentine pesos] each month for you at the school and this makes quite a hole in our margin. Am enclosing, herewith, two pesos [about fifty U.S. cents] which is all that can be spared this month. A suggestion for your Sabbath donations would be about twenty centavos [about five U.S. cents] for Sabbath School, and possibly ten centavos for each of the Church services and ten centavos for the Young People's Society. What do you think of it?

I don't know what I thought of it at the time, but it is worth noting that my father sent fifty cents to his needy son and promptly outlined a plan for how I could give more than 20 percent of it away.

At the same time I was learning an important lesson from my father about fairness. I knew the family was strapped by my school expenses. I was perfectly willing to do my share at school to help out. At the end of one school term I told my father that I wanted to stay at school and work to help with my bill. My father refused. He said that there were poorer students who needed the limited jobs the school could provide. Children of church employees should be supported by their parents or find work elsewhere. Doubt-less, as chairman of the school board, my father was quite aware of how easy it would have been to arrange a job for me. But as an expatriate missionary he also had a keen sense of what was fair, and of the political costs he would have to pay in ill will among the nationals he was attempting to lead.

My father taught me how to work. As a missionary kid living on a mission compound, there wasn't a lot of work I could do outside of the usual chores around a white-collar home. Gardeners took care of the compound grounds, so I never mowed a lawn until after I was married. But because extra cash was very scarce, my father goaded me into small jobs that taught me about responsibility and the world of work. When I was twelve and wanted to buy a bicycle, he helped me launch a chicken business in the back-yard that got me my bicycle and benefited my sisters when I passed the business on to them.

As the proud owner of a self-earned bicycle, I went on to greater things. Street fruit vendors were common in the suburbs of Buenos Aires where we lived. It was an especially good venture for kids who wanted to make a few pesos and yet didn't have the capital for a major overhead expense. Of course, the adults who were in it for a real living had carts and horses, but there was still a place for smaller operators like me and my buddies who were about fourteen or fifteen at the time.

Our biggest problem was getting the fruit from the wholesalers, who were several miles out near the Paraná River delta, to the customers in town. The most obvious way was to ride the train. But that cost a lot of money, or so it seemed to us, and wiped out our profits. Soon enough, however, my buddies discovered something interesting about the railroad companies. They charged half-fare for kids twelve years old and younger. In that culture, puberty for a boy was determined largely by whether he was wearing short pants. I guess they figured no self-respecting teenager would be caught dead wearing short pants, and so the ticket agent never asked ages.

When my buddies started wearing short pants and getting away with half-fare, I was appalled. I talked to my dad. He affirmed me in my quiet outrage. I quit riding the train, attached a larger basket to my bicycle, and began making the fourteen-mile round-trip sojourns out to the wholesalers. I probably didn't make as much money as my buddies did and I had to work a lot harder. But I had a clearer conscience and didn't have to wear short pants. Big money was okay, but it wasn't worth the guilt and self-inflicted disgrace.

After the end of the school term when I was sixteen, Dad got me a job as a mason's tender on a construction job across the city. Work began at 7:00 A.M., which meant that I had to leave home at 5:00 A.M. to take the bus. I earned four pesos a day and transportation costs were again eating into my wages. So I began making the ten-mile one-way trips on my trusty bicycle. I had never had to work very hard before, and that masonry job helped me understand what it meant to be efficient. Under the guidance of one of the older masons, a seventy-year-old man who saw that I had a willing spirit, I learned what I could do. He'd push me, saying, "Keep active. Keep those bricks watered. Keep the mortar coming." The standard formula suggested that a mason's helper could tend about one-and-a-half masons. It wasn't long before my old friend had me handling three. Naturally, the bosses were pleased.

When we came home on furlough in 1939, my father knew that I would stay in the United States when the rest of the family returned to South America a year later. I would start college soon and he wanted me to have some ability to pay my way. His missionary salary would contribute very little to the cost of my private college education at his alma mater.

He had heard that linotype operators could readily find jobs, so he paid a local printer to let me show up at the print shop every day after school to learn the printing business. That knowledge qualified me to attend linotype school in Chicago, which my dad paid for, in the summer of 1940. Perhaps, more than anything else, that one skill, related as it is to the general field of communication, put me on the path that led me into philanthropy.

Although my father had been largely responsible for preparing me for a life of hard work, my mother was perhaps more influential in determining what that work would be.

She insisted that my early years in a foreign country not handicap my facility in my native tongue. Intent on sending me to church schools, she had to face the fact that they were taught exclusively in Spanish. To be certain that I received a good grounding in English, she taught me at home for the first year. Second grade and half of third grade were spent at home in the States on furlough, and she taught me at home for the last half of third grade. She didn't entrust me to the Spanish schools until I entered fourth grade. Thereafter, she alternated my program year by year through the eight grades of my elementary schooling: one at home in English, one at school in Spanish.

As my English developed strongly, despite growing up in a Spanish culture, my mother balanced my program with her desire that I also be thoroughly fluent in Spanish. In 1938 my family was due for a furlough, after which I would remain in the States. My parents decided to postpone the furlough; among other reasons, they wanted me to have one more year in Argentinean schools to polish my command of my second language.

These were the great blessings my parents gave
me: strong religious values and the philanthropic
impulse, an appreciation of hard work and the basic
principles of money management, a values-oriented
education, and a firm grounding in two world languages. America would be a better place today if all
parents could give their kids half as much.

Murray's parents also gave him something else, something so basic that for Murray it may be an a priori assumption. They inspired in him a loyalty and commitment to the
goals and purposes of the religious organization in which he
was nurtured. Murray is a member of the Seventh-day Adventist Church, an evangelical Protestant denomination with
750,000 members in North America and more than six million
members worldwide. Since its organization in the 1860s, the
Adventist Church has placed great emphasis on health care
and education. The *1990 Yearbook of American and Canadian
Churches* (Abingdon Press, 1990, p. 107) notes that Adventists
operate the largest worldwide Protestant educational system
and a large fleet of hospitals in the United States and overseas.

It would not be correct to say that Murray's church has
fully and effectively tapped the potential of philanthropic support for its huge network of service institutions. However,
through Murray's influence, the church is rapidly gaining recognition in fundraising circles as a promoter of the philanthropic
spirit in American society. Murray's calendar is responsible for
much of that recognition. In addition, Adventists are the only
church body represented on the board of NSFRE's National
Philanthropy Day Committee. In an essay on the history of
philanthropy, James Fisher (Fisher and Quehl, 1989, p. 19),
president emeritus of CASE, noted with incredulity the paucity
of apparent academic interest in "perhaps our most unique
national characteristic." He exclaimed: "Not one university
has a division of philanthropy! In fact, this review unearthed
only one institution with anything of that nature: The International Headquarters of the Seventh-day Adventist Church has a
Department of Philanthropic Services."

That department, of course, was founded and has been directed for nearly two decades by Murray. Although Murray's name is inextricably linked with the organization to which he has devoted himself, that organization has only provided the context for his developing stature as an elder statesman in the broader philanthropic world. His professional vision is not limited by parochialism. On the contrary, his parochial interests have made his broader vision possible.

To better appreciate what follows in this book, the reader will find it helpful to be familiar with a brief outline of Murray's professional career. It falls naturally into four eras. During the first era, 1949 to 1961, he founded a fledgling public relations program at what was then the largest medical school west of the Mississippi—the College of Medical Evangelists (CME), now Loma Linda University, in Loma Linda, California. In so doing, he pioneered the concept of institutional public relations and development for the Seventh-day Adventist Church, which even then was operating a substantial collection of hospitals and colleges in the United States and around the world.

Murray started at the bottom. Administrators at the medical school and its parent organization were highly skeptical of the need for "public relations" and "development," concepts rapidly coming into vogue in American higher education after World War II. When the board, pestered by one or two progressive faculty members, grudgingly approved Murray's appointment, it allowed him only half-time employment, subject to a four-month review.

Murray began by churning out news releases, dreaming up science and medical exhibits to bring schoolchildren to campus, giving campus tours, and quietly winning the respect of teachers and administrators for his professional competence and the importance of his work. In the twelve years Murray remained at Loma Linda, he built his shop from one half-time salary into a full-function public relations operation with eighteen full-time employees.

At Loma Linda, Murray immediately began to involve himself in professional growth activities, taking postgraduate classes, attending seminars, and visiting public relations shops at other institutions. He took on regional leadership roles in the American College Public Relations Association (ACPRA), a forerunner of CASE. Through that professional exposure and involvement, Murray's eyes were opened to the burgeoning postwar growth of sophisticated fundraising programs in American higher education and health care.

Pioneers rarely have an easy time, and Murray's experience proved the rule. He pressed the case for a broader vision at Loma Linda but received only tepid support. Administrators, prone to institutional myopia and the victims of exaggerated claims in the past, saw few of the possibilities that other schools were already efficiently tapping.

Disappointed—even frustrated—that his church organization refused to see the light, Murray left Loma Linda in 1961 to work for the G. A. Brakeley Company, and later for the Ford Foundation. His premeditated and publicly announced purpose during this six-year hiatus from church employment—the second era of his career—was to give himself the professional credentials and standing that would win church leaders' enthusiasm for organized philanthropic support programs. With solid experience from Brakeley, Murray moved to Mexico, commissioned by the Ford Foundation to establish a development program at the Autonomous University of Guadalajara. The experiment proved highly successful, the first office of its kind at any private institution of higher education in Latin America.

Murray's third era began in 1967, when, according to his plan, his credentials earned through Brakeley and the Ford Foundation won for organized fundraising the acceptance he desired from his church. Despite significant prodding from several directions, he refused to attach himself to any one hospital or college as a development director. His vision saw the need for a central consulting service that would pull all system institutions along into the world of philanthropic support. He negotiated a position with his church's regional administrative unit in the Mid-Atlantic states as a consultant for institutional development. During this era he consulted extensively for a variety of institutions in Latin America and conducted a key campaign for a small church-operated hospital in Hackettstown, New Jersey. That campaign helped break most of his church's administrative resistance to his ideas and paved the way for broadening the application of his vision.

The year 1973 marked the beginning of the fourth era, in which Murray established himself at Adventist World Headquarters in Washington, D.C., as director of Philanthropic Service for Institutions. In that office he helps nurture and establish programs among more than one hundred church institutions located primarily in the continental United States. Among his major accomplishments were several campaigns for new hospitals and the establishment of challenge programs for alumni of church-related colleges and secondary schools. The office has also given him the platform from which he has launched some of his most important initiatives on behalf of his profession, including his "Giving Is Caring" page-a-day calendar and his persistent campaign for a postage stamp celebrating the philanthropic spirit in American life.

For Murray, it has been a long road, but one he has traveled with unconquerable zest and determination. As a young man fresh out of college in 1949, he heard much about the futility of believing that his church's institutions would ever have any use for professional public relations and philanthropy. He took the rebuke as a personal challenge and proved the rascals wrong. Moreover, he established his own name and, thereby, that of his church as a recognized leader in the philanthropic world.

He made a community for himself. And he has made a life.

 2

A Month in the Life of an Effective Philanthropic Fundraiser

Blessed is he who has found his work; let him ask no other business.
—*Thomas Carlyle,* Past and Present, *Book III, chap. 11*

"Sometimes people envy me because I travel a lot," says Milton Murray. "They're tied to a desk in an office job. Their work hardly takes them out of the building, let alone out of town. So they think that flying around the country would be exciting. Geographical name dropping would make them feel important. And it probably would be exciting—for about the first two months. And then it would become simply a duty, then a nuisance, and then a burden. That's when the real test comes. Can you put up with it week after week, month after month? And more importantly: can you discipline yourself to produce 'on the run'?"

For the occasional tourist, airports exude an aura of excitement and adventure. But for chronic business travelers, including many philanthropy professionals, it's a different story. Airports are high-stress places: the frustration caused by dealing with lost luggage, unapologized-for delays, crowds, cramped seating, and mediocre food can take its toll on normal stamina.

It has little noticeable effect on Milton Murray.

He appears as much at work in an airport or in the air as in his office. Pay phones, mail slots, airline frequent flyer lounges, postcard racks, and now FAX machines, he asserts, constantly prod him with opportunities and become the tools of his productivity: a quick call to a donor, a card of congratulations to a volunteer, a FAX to his secretary or a staffer, or perhaps a scribbled memo to himself about a new way to market his page-a-day philanthropy calendars.

In *Born to Raise*, Jerold Panas (1988, p. 131) describes in succinct and poignant detail the Milton Murray dozens of other great fundraisers have come to know:

> One of my lasting memories of Milton Murray is of a late evening flight I took on a blustery February day. I arrived at Chicago's O'Hare Airport past midnight. I was the picture of the worn and weary traveler. Unkempt, rumpled suit, and beaten to the bone.
>
> Coming off the plane, I spotted Milton in the waiting room, surrounded by papers. A worn, bulging leather briefcase by his side, overflowing. He had one of those long yellow tablets he was writing on, whistling and working. He was obviously having a magnificent time, doing what he enjoyed most—working. Oblivious to everyone, he was up to his elbows in paper and work. No lost time, no lost motion. I touched his shoulder and broke the concentration. Ten minutes of uninterrupted discourse followed on his latest pet-project. There's always a pet-project. He makes even a workaholic like me feel lazy. He's an inspiration. I left, feeling ten feet tall.

At nearly seventy years of age, Murray seems to pay the rigors of business travel no more mind than handing a memo to his secretary or reaching for the telephone. Even as this chapter was written, he was on a complex itinerary that allowed him five nights out of thirty to sleep in his own bed at home. It started on a Sunday afternoon, when he was driven to Dulles International Airport for a nonstop flight to Los Angeles. He spent two days in Irvine with one of his favorite donors, playing dual roles as fundraiser and gift adviser. On Tuesday evening he drove back to Los Angeles International Airport for a night flight to Denver and a Wednesday board meeting of the foundation that bears his name.

All day Thursday he met with a select group of development officers from a consortium of hospitals and schools, in what he calls a strategic planning committee. Murray organized it several years ago to dream up new ideas and projects to advance the cause of philanthropy in the consortium of institutions for which he is responsible. The group also provides an annual, informal structure of professional accountability or "peer review" for Murray and his youthful office staff.

After the meeting on Thursday afternoon, he was back on a plane, heading for Dulles and a 9:00 P.M. arrival. He arrived at his house by 11:00 P.M. At 7:00 A.M. Friday morning, as the night security guards were just leaving their shifts, Murray was at his desk at the Adventist World Headquarters, answering mail, writing memos to his staff, compiling statistics, and clipping news items to send to interested donors.

On Saturday, which for Murray is his weekly Sabbath, he attended the Beltsville Seventh-day Adventist Church, a seven-hundred-member congregation, with his wife Virginia and daughter Deanne. Then, in keeping with his lifelong custom, he spent a quiet afternoon relaxing at home, reading devotional literature, napping occasionally, and typing the general family letter he mails every week to his son, sisters, cousins, aunts, and close personal friends—seventeen in all.

When the sun set on this typical Saturday, ending Murray's Sabbath, he spread out paperwork on the round table in his small kitchen and began to refine his itinerary for the next two weeks, make phone calls, and write letters until well past midnight. Five hours later, at 6:00 A.M., he was in his office, doing more of the same.

Murray takes seriously the directive in the Fourth Commandment: "Six days shalt thou labor and do all thy work." After his quiet relaxation on Saturday, he puts Sunday to use much like any other workday, although he makes some adjustments.

"They say that Henry Ford used to claim, in a burst of esthetic broadmindedness, that his customers could have any color Model T they wanted, as long as it was black," says Murray. "Well, my wife tells me something similar about Sundays. She says I can be at the office just as long as I want on Sunday mornings, as long as I'm home for the day by 9:00 A.M."

On this particular Sunday, he missed the deadline and didn't make it home until ten o'clock. After a quick breakfast, he went out to mow the lawn, the last chance he'd have for three weeks. Because of rain the day before, he found the grass still too wet to mow, so he drove the two miles back to the office to help one of his staff members organize the collating, packaging, and mailing of back orders on one of Murray's philanthropy publications.

When he returned home, the grass had dried and he mowed the lawn, finishing at two o'clock. After two more quick trips back to the office to pick up items he had uncharacteristically forgotten, he arrived home to finish packing; the company car and driver were in his driveway, waiting to take him to Washington National Airport for his late-afternoon flight to Miami and then on to São Paulo, Brazil.

Decades of travel experience have taught Murray to reduce his luggage requirements. He is not, by usual corporate executive standards, a flashy dresser, so his travel wardrobe, even for an extended trip, might consist of a pair of slacks, one sport coat, three shirts, one tie, one suit, and one pair of shoes. Most of the time, he gambles on the amenities that he hopes hotels will supply, so his kit consists of little more than a razor and a toothbrush. At one point in his career, when he was directing three campaigns, he kept a suit and extra shirt at his regular stop in Texas, a raincoat in Oregon, and a pair of overshoes in Michigan.

Sometimes, when he's on a short trip of one or two nights, Murray relies on slightly unorthodox methods to avoid the burden of a suitcase or garment bag. Some of his colleagues at Andrews University still regale themselves with the story, doubtless improved with age, of how Murray showed up in the administrative suite for a consulting appointment with the vice president for development. While searching for a document in his attaché case, he effected only mild embarrassment in front of the vice president and secretary when his underwear tumbled out.

His packing finished, Murray sat down at the kitchen table for a snack. When Virginia pointed out, with growing concern for his flight schedule, that the driver was waiting for him, Murray said, "I've still got five minutes. Our appointment was for 4:00. It's only 3:55."

"He always uses every minute," Virginia says. "He'll work, or accomplish something important on his agenda, right up to the moment when he absolutely has to do something else. He's very efficient with his time, always planning and using it carefully." Murray strode out to the driveway at the appointed time for his ride to the airport.

Twenty hours later, at 11:00 A.M. the next day, he arrived in São Paulo, Brazil, for an eleven-day itinerary in South America. He spent Monday through Thursday at an ill-heated youth camp on the Atlantic Ocean lecturing in Spanish for several hours a day to a group of religious and educational leaders on the philosophy and practice of philanthropy and fundraising. On Friday he traveled to Buenos Aires, Argentina, where, on Saturday, he preached the sermon at one of the principal Adventist churches in the city. Saturday night, he addressed a group of sixty business leaders about philanthropy. Sunday through Wednesday, he repeated his lecture series, this time to a group of religious and educational leaders assembled on a college campus in the interior of Argentina.

On Thursday he began the long journey back to Washington, D.C., arriving at noon on Friday to meet with the president of the Adventist World Headquarters. Murray had drawn up the agenda for the meeting on the plane over the Amazon and dictated it to his secretary from a pay phone in Miami between planes. On Friday and Saturday nights, he relished the luxury of his own bed. He spent Saturday morning at church in Beltsville with his family, relaxed in the afternoon, and then performed his usual Saturday night and Sunday morning routine at the kitchen table and in the office.

On Sunday afternoon he boarded a plane in Baltimore for the six-hour journey to Vancouver, British Columbia, to meet with a major foundation on Monday. On Monday evening he flew to San Francisco to attend the annual conference of the AHP on Tuesday and Wednesday. He then drove two hours north to Pacific Union College in Angwin, California, where, on Thursday morning, he conducted what he calls a "development audit." On these visits, he meets individually with a college's alumni, public relations, and development officers to evaluate each department's responsibility and effectiveness in implementing the school's overall advancement program.

A flight instructor from the college flew Murray back to San Francisco on Thursday afternoon, so that he could make a connecting flight to Eugene, Oregon, for a dinner appointment with a donor who had generously supported some of Murray's college and high school challenge programs. On Friday morning the donor drove him to the airport, where Murray began a succession of flights that took him to Seattle, Dallas, and Saint Louis, where he rented a car and drove to Decatur, Illinois. There, he met up with Virginia, who had just arrived in Decatur by plane from Baltimore. The couple joined the rest of Virginia's family, who had assembled in their hometown for a reunion on Saturday and Sunday morning. On Sunday afternoon Milton and Virginia boarded their separate flights back to Washington National Airport.

Thirty days. Twenty-four thousand miles. Fourteen hours of professional lecturing. Twenty-two hours of meetings. One sermon. Thirty-two business letters. One hundred twenty-five personal, handwritten postcards to campaign volunteers. One hundred handwritten postscript notes to college classmates (he is a class agent) on letters forwarded to him in Decatur by the college alumni office in California. Eighteen different beds. Sixty-eight-and-a-half years old.

Murray is used to schedules that put him in different hotels, motels, college residence halls, or private homes eight or ten nights in a row. His personal record occurred in March 1971, when he racked up thirteen consecutive overnighters in Dayton, Ohio; Pittsburgh, Pennsylvania; Hackettstown, New Jersey; Persippany, New Jersey; San Juan, Puerto Rico; two different guest rooms in Mayaguez, Puerto Rico; Dallas–Fort Worth Airport; Keene, Texas; Burleson, Texas; Kansas City, Kansas; Shawnee Mission, Kansas; and Chicago, Illinois.

Many highly successful philanthropy professionals and other business travelers can readily identify with Murray's schedule. They can take the stress and produce on the run. But most of them probably have not kept detailed records to prove it. In twenty-two years as a philanthropy consultant, from January 1968 to March 1990, Murray logged more than 2.5 million air miles on commercial airlines, a distance roughly equivalent to five round trips to the moon. A lover of oddball statistics, Murray notes that, put another way, his air log shows him traveling one mile for every minute of every working hour, eight hours a day, five days a week, forty-eight working weeks a year, for those twenty-two years. In other words, Murray's working pace is a neat, literal illustration of the old expression "going a mile a minute." And this figure doesn't include ground transportation. He estimates that he drives a modest average of three thousand business miles each year and rides trains and subways for hundreds more.

Murray finds the time to make some of his travel arrangements himself, and he generally feels better when he does. He returned to the office recently, pounding the desk and fuming over the "narrow-mindedness" of the corporate travel service he had trusted with his itinerary. According to Murray, the guilty travel agent had scheduled him, in the middle of a perfectly usable business day, for a three-hour layover in an airport somewhere between Columbus, Ohio, and Baltimore.

"They probably did it to save a lousy $80," he said in disgust.

Murray lowered his voice as he made his pronouncement, as much for symbolic reasons as literal ones. As an executive for a religious organization that is entirely dependent on the cheerful and sacrificial giving of its members, Murray cannot afford to be branded a spendthrift—particularly as a fundraiser. And, indeed, his reputation is exactly the opposite. Few of Murray's corporate colleagues would choose to spend as many business travel nights as he does in the private homes of friends, costing the organization nothing, rather than enjoying the comfort of well-appointed motels or hotels at $60 to $70 a night.

On the other hand, Murray's time is money. The travel agent might think that the office has been saved $80, but Murray's time as a consultant to a large consortium of church-run colleges and hospitals requires a corporate investment of about $500 a day and is probably worth two to three times that amount in terms of results. Yet Murray does not receive a consultant's usual remuneration. He is paid a flat salary from his organization that works out to about $140 a day for the 231 business days of the year.

Those who know him well would guess that Murray's obvious annoyance over the lost time was probably directed as much at himself as at the travel agent. His own poor planning, as he would describe it, had left him unprepared to put the surprise layover to its most efficient use.

That doesn't happen often. In June 1989, Murray was hospitalized for a crushed disk, with the inevitable surgery and slow recovery. It required little apparent mental effort or imagination for Murray to convert his hospital bed—fully rigged with traction equipment—into a desk, and his semi-private room into an office. Professional colleagues, donors, fundraising volunteers, prospective calendar buyers, or contacts in Murray's incessant campaign for a postage stamp honoring philanthropy all received his business-as-usual calls and marveled to learn that he was flat on his back.

"Typical of how he operates, Milton called me once and I heard a lot of noise in the background," recalls Ernest Wood, a consultant for the Russ Reid Company in Pasadena and 1989 winner of the Outstanding Fund-Raising Executive of the Year Award from NSFRE. "I said, 'Milton, where *are* you?' And he said, 'Oh, I'm at a pay phone here on the sidewalk. Something's wrong with my car, and they're going to be a while fixing it, so I'm taking advantage of the thirty-minute wait to get some of this work done.' And so there he was, going through his phone lists on the sidewalk, calling people. It's unbelievable. He just keeps pushing."

Recently Murray was selected to be on call for a week of jury duty, which required him to show up each morning for possible jury selection. The process knocked out the major part of every working day. Murray worked around it by arriving at his office to work at 6:00 A.M. before reporting to the courthouse. When he was released, sometimes late in the afternoon, he returned directly to the office and worked into the evening.

The mass of handwritten notes he churned out during the thirty-day itinerary outlined above is a Murray trademark. For several years he served as national chairman of NSFRE's Every Member campaign for the annual professional development fund. Typically, he would send out several mailings a year to the annual fund's officers in the society's 101 chapters across the nation. In 1990, for example, he sent them all personal postcards from Austria, Germany, or Hungary during a two-week business trip to Europe in May. In September, all 101 received cards that he wrote in Brazil, in Argentina, or on the plane back to Miami.

With his November mailing, Murray even managed to impress himself. He had arrived at Los Angeles International Airport at 7:30 P.M. for a late-evening, overnight flight to Dulles. By the time he heard his plane called at 10:20, he had written forty-four cards. He gave them to the Red Carpet Club attendant to mail later. Once settled on the plane, he resumed his writing for an hour and a half, then closed his briefcase and dozed. Two hours later he awoke and wrote for an hour before the plane landed at Dulles at 5:30 A.M. He found a mailbox in the Dulles terminal and stuffed in the forty-one new cards he had completed on the flight. On the fifty-minute ride to his home he forfeited his usual chatter with the company driver for the sake of writing sixteen more cards, which he dropped in the mailbox at the end of his driveway. One hundred and one postcards in eight hours, including sleep time, from Los Angeles to Beltsville. After a hot shower and breakfast at home he made it to his office by 8:15.

Murray is a firm believer in the power of the personal touch. Many executives, understandably, avoid the task of putting a personal, original signature on stacks of otherwise impersonal letters. Murray welcomes it, turning the chore into an opportunity to make genuine personal contact by laboriously writing meaningful notes at the bottom. It takes energy and careful planning, because Murray usually does the work in odd and easily wastable moments in the evenings and on weekends. Over the July 4 holiday weekend in 1991, Murray handwrote more than a hundred personal notes to NSFRE chapter presidents, alerting them to the latest good news in his campaign for the philanthropy stamp and—as always—soliciting their support. "Sure," he explains, "I could have had my secretary prepare a form letter. But I can guarantee that my personal, handwritten note had a much greater impact, demanded more attention, and got better results. Personal communication is always that way. Of course it's easier to let the word processor or photocopier do it all for you, but there is a price to pay. And for much of what I do, I'm not willing to pay that price. My message is important, and I'll take the extra trouble to see that it gets through loud and clear."

Of course, Murray is fully aware of, and exploits, the manners and value of proper business communication. Yet he gives much less credence than most to the necessity of putting every written communication in the form of a neatly typed business letter on proper stationery. He is much more concerned with making his point quickly and efficiently than with having a photocopy for the file. Thus, he is not hindered by the effort, equipment, and process of dictation, transcription, editing, typing, and copying that often go into even casual memos. This frees him up mentally to be more creative, spontaneous, and productive in maintaining close contacts, the very substance of his vocation.

Whatever mental benefits may accrue from his personal work style, what holds him together physically? Fervent advocates of the gospel of fitness may be annoyed by exhibits like Murray.

"What do I do for exercise? Well, let's see. [Long pause] I mow the lawn. I guess that's it."

Murray claims no interest in sports or athletic games. He's tried to play tennis twice and has been hounded into an occasional game of volleyball on company picnics. He hates walking for the sake of walking, even though he admits that this latest fitness fad might provide the opportunity for valuable creative thinking.

"I do my creative thinking in bed at about 3:30 in the morning when I can't sleep. So what's the point of taking extra time to go walking? I can be much more productive when I'm sitting at my desk writing than when I'm walking and 'thinking.'"

As an Adventist, Murray grew up in a tradition where significant emphasis was placed on healthful living, including a good diet and plenty of regular exercise. A clear failure in the exercise category, Murray's lifelong vegetarian diet might be the explanation for an astonishing record of good health. He claims that, with the exception of a seven-week period in 1989 when he was out of the office recovering from back surgery, his total lost work time due to illness, in a career spanning more than forty years, amounts to one afternoon. That was thirty-five years ago when he caught a bad cold. He says, "I don't want to give the impression that I never get the sniffles. Sure, I catch a little cold once in a while, or get a headache, like everyone else. But I don't see any need for that to get in the way of my work. I figure I can feel miserable at the office, getting something done, just as well as I can feel miserable at home getting nothing done. So for me, it's the office."

In light of his nonexistent exercise program, Murray may be a quirk of nature—a nonsmoking, nondrinking, vegetarian variation of the archetypal 103-year-old who claims that the secret to the good life rests in two packs a day and three good belts before noon. This may be the only explanation for his iron constitution, his unflagging energy, and his apparent workaholism. But Murray plays coy on the workaholism charge.

> Isn't workaholism an addiction to work? I'm not addicted to work. I'm addicted to fun. I enjoy and get pleasure and recreation out of what I get paid to do. Other people go to the beach for recreation. I go to the office. I'm not a workaholic. I'm a funaholic. I suppose that by the standards of the people who are bored with their jobs, who barely get to work on time, who can hardly wait till the clock strikes five to get out of there—yes, by that standard, I'd be a workaholic. If they found themselves forced to put in the time I do, life would be a living hell.
>
> Those who wish to get into fundraising must understand that to be fully successful and on the cutting edge will require a reasonably high degree of energy. Fundraising requires creativity, but your creativity will accomplish nothing if you don't have the energy and determination to execute those bright little ideas: an appropriate gift or meaningful follow-up after a visit with an important donor, a letter to a new networking contact you met at a convention, or a new argument to justify to skeptical superiors the purchase of the new computer equipment your staff so desperately needs. These creative ideas often occur at odd moments sometime between the evening news and deep sleep. The fundraiser who is destined to succeed

is the one who is at the office at 6:45 the next morning, clicking away on a keyboard. And that takes simple energy, and good doses of it.

Murray readily acknowledges that he is "not the world's greatest delegator" and admits that his weakness in that area may place more demands on his own time. All the same, he feels strongly that most young fundraisers aiming for real success won't be very familiar with a forty-hour week. His opinion is based on a broad generalization about the status of philanthropic fundraising in nonprofit organizations and institutions in the United States.

I don't know any really successful fundraisers who are "eight-to-five" people. I suppose there are some, but I've never met them. And I don't think there will be many for quite a while.

What do I mean? I mean that even today, huge numbers of development people have to continue to justify their positions. This is particularly true in the thousands of church-related colleges, hospitals, and social service agencies across the country. They have administrations, or at least boards, that even today may not recognize the full potential of philanthropic support and the value of having a staff to go after it.

Consider a college, for example. Everybody knows that a college must have a library. The library is the heart of academic life. With all the tradition and technology of library science firmly in place in American academia, it's quite likely that a head librarian can work a forty-hour week. Maybe even less. Nobody's going to say, "Hey, we don't need a librarian."

Not so with thousands of college development offices. Anxious administrators, looking for immediate bottom-line results in tight times, have little patience for spending salary money for long-term results that only will reflect well on their successors. So for thousands of fundraisers, there is the constant tension of proving their worth. In effect, they have to do two jobs. First, they have to build the idea in the minds of administrators and the board that development is a function that has an important role to play in the college. And second, they have to keep producing something to validate what they've been advocating. That takes energy and stamina.

Of course, there are shining exceptions like Harvard, Stanford, Notre Dame, and a hundred other schools where the development function has become as institutionalized as the library. The eight-to-five guy will be happier there, but the chances are slim he'll land such a job without having proved himself in a more typical setting.

When I started the public relations and development function at Loma Linda University forty years ago, I found myself spending the equivalent of a half-time job in activities designed simply to sell the concept internally and justify my existence. Not only did I have to get the school's name in the paper, bring groups to campus, and make friends in the community, but I had to convince the board and many of the administrators that those things were really good for the institution. They didn't believe in me, and they didn't believe in fundraising or public relations. I was working with a bunch of "unbelievers." There was no context of support, no institutional ethos or inertia in place upon which I could build. So I had a job and a half. It takes a lot of creative energy to keep that up day in and day out.

Then I went to work for Brakeley, with the same skills and the same intelligence. And it was a whole new world. I worked on a campaign for a consortium of five hospitals in Phoenix, Arizona. The campaign board was stacked with all kinds of heavy-hitter community leaders: bank presidents, corporate officers of major manufacturing plants, heads of local utilities companies. They wanted more hospital beds in Phoenix and they knew that they had to raise four to five million dollars to get them. In that context I had many other forces supporting me—from above, beside me, and below—in the goal of raising money.

So I only had to work about seven hours a day, and I was still moving like greased lightning. My colleagues at Brakeley thought I was a human dynamo, and I thought I was on vacation. I didn't have to argue or explain or convince anybody that we needed to fund a mailing or put out a publication. I was *told* to put out a publication. I didn't have to argue about budgets. I just did the work. It was heaven.

If you are a young professional, you must recognize that even today, you may find yourself in a context similar to mine at Loma Linda University thirty-five years ago. You may be in a small hospital, a small college, or a small social service agency somewhere. You will discover, to your surprise, that the frontiers of philanthropy are still to be conquered in this country.

You will have to be a pioneer. If you are going to make it, you'd better love being a pioneer, and you'd better have the requisite energy, stamina, and efficiency. Because pioneers don't work eight to five.

3

Answering the Call:
Finding a Career
in Philanthropy

The lines are fallen unto me in pleasant places;
yea, I have a goodly heritage.
                                    —*Psalms 16:6*

How did it happen? And how does it happen?

What motivated Milton Murray, as a young man fresh out of college, to move into an embryonic profession that was often grossly misunderstood by society, and that sometimes still is? What attracts people to this occupation today? Is nonprofit public relations and philanthropic fundraising a profession one can fall into by accident? Should it be? Are there any lessons that young people of today, also fresh out of college and straining for a life purpose, may learn from Murray's experience? Can his experience help to point, affirm, or explain—if not smooth—the way into the profession he has found so rewarding?

29

Murray, in an informal way, answers some of these questions, first by facing facts and then by sharing a little of his story.

It's become a humorous cliché in our culture, but we still like to ask children: what do you want to be when you grow up? We hear the usual answers: doctor, lawyer, merchant, thief, or president of the United States. The list of possibilities understandable and attractive to the childhood imagination gets longer all the time, largely dependent on which occupations happen to be getting good press in popular culture. Refreshingly, you'll find some kids who are motivated by an altruistic spirit and want to do something in the service professions, such as teaching, nursing, the ministry, or the social sciences. But I have yet to hear an eight-year-old declare for a career as a philanthropic fundraiser.

Of course, as an eight-year-old or an eighteen-year-old, I wouldn't have declared for it either. Neither would many college students of today. It's not on the hot list. Even though the typical college student changes majors two or three times, it's unlikely that the search for purpose will end, during the college years, on a track headed directly for nonprofit public relations and philanthropic fundraising.

I don't expect things to change in the near future. Part of the explanation is that philanthropic fundraising has only begun to define itself as a profession in the past thirty years or so. Even today, higher education in the United States is just beginning to recognize it as a specialty within the broad area of communications. Another important factor is that, unlike some of the other service-oriented professions, nonprofit public relations and philanthropic fundraising, by its very nature, will never get much press.

In our society, it takes celebrities, created by mass media, to make a profession recognizable and attractive to an eight-year-old or an eighteen-year-old. It is no discredit to Mother Teresa or the great humanitarian nature of her work to acknowledge that she is a celebrity. Through her example, highly and rightly publicized throughout our society, thousands may be inspired to answer similar callings. Popular psychologists like Joyce Brothers or James Dobson become celebrities by finding ways of providing their services to the masses. Even the ministry achieves celebrity status, some of it negative, through televised religion and related scandals.

Can philanthropic fundraising achieve celebrity status in our society? I doubt it. There is little apparent visceral or emotional drama in the work. No life-and-death moments in an emergency room. No spellbinding summations to a jury. No tearful calls to repentance. Of course, there are big gifts and successful campaigns. But for the fundraiser those are usually only moments of private triumph. Other people—the CEOs and the donors—get most of the credit, as they should.

If philanthropic fundraising could be romanticized or glamorized, we might hear more from the eight-year-olds. Or we might hear more college students declaring that they want to be vice president for development at a major university or hospital. Yet even an altruistic teenager is much more likely to consider a career running soup kitchens than a career raising money to make those soup kitchens possible. And I doubt that glamorization would do much for the profession. More likely, it would undermine the quiet trust and credibility upon which the profession rests. It also inevitably would attract individuals who were in it for the wrong reasons.

I suspect that for years to come, young people will wander into nonprofit public relations work and, ultimately, philanthropic fundraising, much as I did more than forty years ago. But once they get there, they will discover that it is exactly where they were meant to be.

As much as any other influence in his young adult life, the army nudged Murray toward the career he began in 1949 and has pursued with such an intense sense of purpose ever since. Not surprisingly, this point was not obvious to Murray while the army had him, or even when he landed his first public relations job. At the time, it seemed that it all "just sort of happened." More than forty years of refined and focused hindsight has helped him to make some sense of the meandering path that led him to his life calling.

As it was for thousands of other American boys, December 7, 1941, was the day Milton Murray became a man.

I was hanging around the lounge of the men's dorm at Emmanuel Missionary College with six or eight other fellows listening to the radio. That was a rather popular way to kill time, because we weren't allowed to have radios in our rooms. We heard the news about the bombing at Pearl Harbor and we just looked at each other. I suppose we were all thinking: "How does this affect me? I'm nineteen, I'm twenty, I'm twenty-one." We were just kids, but we quickly grasped the obvious implications. It was inevitable that we would be drafted. And even though I maintained a conscientious objection to bearing arms, I was ready to do my part.

He was so ready, in fact, that he allowed the inevitable and imminent prospect of the draft to dominate his life during the next few months. Other aspects of his life, which might resume their normal importance during peacetime, were inconsequential now.

His grades hit bottom. Murray, whose scholastic record was a fine example of the "gentleman's C," never was destined, by any observable academic evidence, for a scholarly life. Yet his report slip for the spring of 1942 showed an exaggerated and almost calculating carelessness about his studies: History of Western Europe—D, Intermediate Accounting—D, General Chemistry—F, Trigonometry—D.

When school was out for the summer, he decided that he wanted to sell books door to door through the church's well-developed literature distribution system. The sales managers sent him to Bad Axe, Michigan, where he boarded in a farmer's home. He remembers, "I lost eighty dollars. That was the grand total of my summer's earnings selling books. The first few days, I walked from farmhouse to farmhouse before I finally figured out that I needed a bicycle. I bought one with four dollars down on some type of payment plan. The bike didn't help much and I barely prevented an even greater financial loss by discovering that migrant Mexicans who worked in the sugar beet fields wanted to buy books in Spanish."

At the end of the summer, eighty dollars poorer than when he'd started, Murray returned to Berrien Springs. Still, the inevitable draft notice had not arrived. It was pointless to start school. With nothing better to occupy his time, he took a full-time job as a linotype operator back at the College Press. When he could stand the waiting no longer, he and a college friend of the same age went down to the draft board and signed up together. With some straightforward and apparently persuasive arguments before the necessary officials, they enlisted as volunteers without forfeiting any of their rights as drafted conscientious noncombatants. They were inducted on October 5, 1942.

They sent us to Camp Grant in Rockford, Illinois, for basic training. As soon as we arrived they assigned us to our barracks and had us make our bunks. I didn't waste any time. A few minutes later, in the middle of all the commotion, one of the corporals walked by my bunk and tossed a quarter on it; the quarter bounced about half an inch. He said, "Hey, fellows, get over here. This soldier knows how to make a bed." I guess that put me in good standing. A few minutes later another corporal grabbed me and four other guys and said, "Come on outside, and I'll teach you how to salute." I already knew how to salute. In fact, I was a few steps ahead of most of the others. At Emmanuel Missionary College I had gone through a training course that the Adventists had run for several years to prepare noncombatants for service as medics. We learned all the basics of getting along in the army and a lot about first aid.

So I already had some orientation to army life. When I got to Camp Grant I stood out from the other recruits. This gave me a certain confidence in myself that allowed me to fit in easily, even though the rest of my rather conservative, straitlaced background might have set me up for the opposite.

In the early spring of 1943, the army shipped Murray to Fort Richardson in Anchorage, Alaska. After ten days of unloading coal sacks in a freight yard in freezing weather, Murray was delighted to be assigned to the 183rd Army Hospital at the fort. Murray waited, primed and ready to work.

We got to the hospital in the morning. They assigned us our bunks and told us to reassemble in the afternoon for our job assignments. At this point I had been in the army for about five months. All I had been doing was "getting ready." I had come out of college ready to do my part to win the war. I wanted to do something besides policing the parade grounds for cigarette butts or cutting lemon pies on KP duty. I kept asking myself, "When are they going to give me something to do for the cause?" Well, the time had come. At last, I was going to get my first real army job.

A sergeant took me down to one of the hospital wards, where I had been assigned. This was exciting. He led me into a utility room and there he showed me a bucket and a pile of old rags. He filled the bucket with water, handed me a rag, pointed, and said, "See that baseboard? That needs some attention."

So my first official job in the army was cleaning baseboards. Frankly, I was more than just a little irritated. I had given up my college education—such as it was—to clean baseboards.

Murray's ability to work conscientiously and to relate easily to his superiors moved him off the irritating baseboard routine soon enough. He became a technician in the ward—acting essentially as a nurse's assistant, giving backrubs, making beds, serving meals, and taking temperatures. Within a short time his superiors, impressed with his efficiency, moved him into the surgery unit.

Murray's industriousness earned him steadily advancing jobs until he was a scrub nurse in major surgery. At about the same time his superiors discovered that he could type. He was dispatched, against his wishes, to the Sick and Wounded Office to handle medical records. While working there he had his first small test of his Saturday Sabbath observance when the warrant officer wasn't willing to give him the whole day off.

He said I could have the morning off for church. I explained that Adventists observe the Sabbath from Friday evening until Saturday evening and that it involves more than just going to church.

He grudgingly agreed, but I told him that if he didn't want to take the responsibility, I would talk to the captain. And if the captain balked, I'd go to the colonel. I was pleasant about it, but he knew there wasn't any possibility for compromise.

I sympathized with his problem. Everyone else in the office had to work Saturday, and at least one person, on rotation, had to cover the office on Sunday. To prove my willingness to work with the system, I put in extra time to learn the operation as quickly as possible. Then I volunteered to cover the office every

Sunday so that the other men never had to work that day. They liked that.

While Murray was making friends in the Sick and Wounded Office, surgery fell short on qualified help. The officer in charge specifically requested Murray back. After a major and unresolved squabble among his superior officers over Murray's work assignment, he found himself in front of the colonel, the chief executive of the entire hospital operation. The colonel surprised everyone by simply letting Murray decide. He returned to the surgery ward.

Murray gained more experience getting along with VIPs in another important way. Each Saturday he attended church in Anchorage, and periodically Eskimos who also attended would tell the congregation of the very real problems they faced with their draft status as noncombatants. "Alaskan noncombatants weren't sent to the two or three basic training camps down in the States that specialized in medical training. They went to regular boot camps in Alaska, where the military establishment wasn't as used to dealing with them, and particularly with those who wanted Saturdays off. Eight or nine times, I took men back to camp, talked to their sergeant or captain, pointed out the clear but little-known regulations, and got the matter settled. It helped my sense of confidence about getting things done."

In addition to his regular army duties, Murray picked up a part-time job at the *Anchorage Times* for three hours a day, five days a week, after completing his hospital shift. His linotyping skills provided the entrée, although he usually ran the bindery. This job, with its daily trips into Anchorage's business district, provided the context for Murray's most significant crisis and learning experience as a soldier. Nearly forty-five years later, his blend of sobriety and whimsy in recounting the episode reveals the milestone it came to be in his young life.

One day my friend George asked me to take some film downtown to have it developed. He rarely had occasion to leave the post, and I went downtown every day. So naturally I agreed. When I dropped the film off at the local pharmacy, I had to leave a name. Since I was the person who would pick up the pictures, I wrote in my own name.

Three or four days later, I signed and paid for the pictures, and took them to George. Later in the evening he said, "You know, something is strange here. I took twenty-four pictures but I only got twenty-three back." It wasn't any big deal to him and we didn't think anything more about it.

About ten days later I received an order to report to the captain. He got right to the point. He said, "Private Murray, you have been charged by the post commander with attempting to develop obscene photographs." Then he produced George's missing picture and dropped it on the desk with a flourish.

Now George was a bit of a character. A few weeks earlier, we had been on a vacation leave to Mount McKinley. At the hotel George must have persuaded one of our buddies to take a picture of him sitting on the toilet. It was a side view. His shirt was hanging down on the side and his pants were bunched up around his knees, so all that was visible were his knees and lower thigh. He was looking at the camera with a silly grin on his face while smoking a fat cigar. The picture may have been a little crude, but it certainly wasn't obscene.

Apparently a petty bureaucrat somewhere along the line brought this "serious matter" to the attention of the commanding general, who advised the VIPs at the army hospital. So here I was, straitlaced Milton Murray, charged as a conspirator in a sinister plot to undermine the morals of the United States Army.

This worried me greatly because it meant a court-martial. It's true that it was at the lowest level, but it was still a court-martial. I had never been in any serious trouble in my life. And now the United States Army was after me.

I went right over and told the whole fearful story to my friends in surgery. They laughed. They thought it was a hilarious joke that Murray, the one guy they regarded as a saint, was up for something like this. Maybe he didn't drink, and he didn't smoke, and he didn't gamble, and he didn't chase women, but at last they had found the weak spot in his armor. Ha! Ha! Ha!

I didn't think it was funny at all. I told my superiors I needed time off from the surgery ward to defend myself. With some amusement, they let me off.

I went over to the Main Post Headquarters and asked to see someone in the legal department. Much to my outrage, they said that they could only help GIs with civilian legal problems back home—like divorce. Because this was a military matter, they could provide no help. Finally, they told me about a lieutenant working in the camp bakery who had just graduated cum laude from Harvard Law School. They said that he probably would have fun helping me.

So I went to see the Harvard baker and told him my story, and he laughed too. But he agreed to help. He talked to the head nurse at the hospital, showed her the picture, and asked, "Do you consider this picture obscene?" She said no. Then he went to the postmaster and asked if he could prosecute anyone for sending that picture through the mails. The postmaster said no. Meanwhile, I went down to the newspaper where I worked and told my friends that I'd probably be post-bound until the trial, so I wouldn't be in to work. That concerned them, because they liked me and they liked my work. They got word to Robert Atwood, the publisher of the paper, who was a friend of the commanding general. By this time, I was a household name in the hospital fraternity. Some of my buddies in surgery who had jobs on the side checking hats and coats at the officers' club put in a few good words for me with the officers. So did the nurses in the hospital who were dating officers. They told the officers, "Look, Murray's the one all the soldiers trust with their money when they gamble. When they get paid, they give him their money—six or seven hundred dollars a night. *He goes to church!*"

About a week before I was to stand trial, the word came down that the general had withdrawn the complaint and I was exonerated. This was a great relief, because I didn't want a court-martial, however trivial, on my record. And if I hadn't pushed, it would have been there.

Now that I look back on it, it was a great experience. This episode, as well as my dealings with superiors about my work and my fight for Sabbath privileges for the Alaskan soldiers, helped me to understand how things get done in an organization. Since then, I've never been afraid to talk to the person at the top, when it is necessary. I'll walk into any office, make friends with secretaries, call executives on the phone at home, do whatever I have to do, and see whomever I have to see to get the work done.

I know that some people are timid about doing this, and to some extent I understand. But my childhood, influenced by my father's work, and these extremely valuable experiences in the army, convinced me that there is no reason to be timid about going up the line, right to the top, to solve a problem or bring about a new idea. Even as a young college student, I was comfortable with people and developed a willingness to talk to anyone. That's one of the most valuable assets I've had in my work in public relations and philanthropy. The nature of the work often requires the young professional to deal with people "in a different league." But somehow I developed the habit of seeing people as people, and it has helped tremendously.

After two years in Alaska, Murray was assigned in May 1945 to Camp Crowder in Missouri, a convenient place from which to pursue a romance in Decatur, Illinois, that had barely begun three years before (and that existed almost exclusively in Murray's mind). Virginia Hudgins had been a copyholder at the College Press and a student at Emmanuel Missionary College in the fall of 1942, when Murray was working there full time as a linotype operator just before entering the army. They had hardly had a conversation before Murray left and had not corresponded once during his stint in the army.

Murray made characteristically efficient use of several weekend leaves from Camp Crowder to Decatur, and the couple became engaged at the end of October. With an honorable discharge from the army on October 31, 1945, Murray promptly headed back to Alaska for a few months to accept a standing job offer he had with Mr. Atwood, publisher of the *Anchorage Times*. He never made it to Anchorage. His ship from Seattle to Anchorage made a stopover in Ketchikan. As Murray strolled the streets for the afternoon, he spotted a sign for a doctor's office and recognized the physician's name as a man he had heard of in Anchorage. True to a developing habit that has become a Murray trademark, he walked into the office just to say hello.

> Once I got in the doctor's office he never let me go. He said, "Where are you going?" I answered, "I'm going up to Anchorage to work on the *Anchorage Times* for a few months." He said, "Why don't you stay here? I know the editor of the *Ketchikan Chronicle*."
>
> When I protested, he persisted and said, "Please, just go down there and see Bill Baker." So I did. Baker asked me what I could do and I said I was a linotype operator.
>
> "A linotype operator?" Baker said. "I want you to meet the superintendent." So we were introduced and they gave me a job. They had me set a lot of editorials and features that were written well in advance of

deadline. This was fortunate because my linotyping skills were pretty rusty. I probably would have washed out quickly if they had made me set hard news on a short deadline. I worked the evening shift, which was supposed to run from 5:00 P.M. to midnight. I started out by working thirteen hours a night, quitting just before the next shift came on in the morning; however, I only turned in eight hours of time because I knew, to be fair, that I needed to get back up to speed. I did this for the first week I had the job, until I had linotyping down pat again.

I don't want to be too hard on young people these days, because I know I'm an old-timer. But I think that if they really want to produce, they should be willing to spend three or four extra hours a day for a week or a month until they really get a grasp of their job. I don't have much patience with the green kids coming into this work, or any other, right out of college, not knowing anything, and yet thinking they have arrived and can live the life of a seasoned executive.

One of my fundraising colleagues at a large hospital recently told me of a young person he just hired—regrettably—who quickly informed everyone in the office that he didn't work past five o'clock. That kind of attitude, of course, just about assures that he will never really be a success. I realize I may be a little extreme in some of the hours I choose to put into my work, and I'm sure my wife would have appreciated more balance. That's my problem, and one I'll just have to live with. But successful public relations and philanthropy work is a demanding job that can't be packaged into a neat eight-to-five day. If you're not willing to work and really put your organization before yourself, get out of the way and make room for someone who is.

Murray's job on the *Ketchikan Chronicle* opened his eyes to a new professional world, a world quite accessible with the skills, experience, and personality traits he already possessed. His family's extensive personal letter-writing habits had given him an understanding of, and a liking for, the discipline of writing, however unsophisticated it may have been in that form. He mixed easily with people, made friends and contacts almost effortlessly, and wasn't afraid to talk with "big shots." And he learned how social attitudes and understanding were influenced by special events and by the newspaper.

I learned a lot from Bill Baker, the editor. He told me many stories that helped me learn how a community operates and how opinion is shaped. I was impressed with his story of how he had just spent a weekend with the governor of Alaska to talk about the fishing industry in Ketchikan. At that time, Ketchikan was the center of a huge fishing industry. There were some problems affecting the industry that they wanted to bring to the attention of President Truman. The two men decided to see Truman, but they needed some way to draw attention to their visit. So they secured a huge swordfish, packed it in ice, and shipped it from Ketchikan to Washington, D.C., to arrive at the White House at the time of their visit. And of course, in those days, that made a great photograph for the newspapers, which gave good publicity to the bigger story. And Truman followed through. Baker's little story made a great impression on me. I was just twenty-four or twenty-five years old and hadn't even finished college. I had never thought much about how things came to public notice. It hadn't occurred to me that opinion could be influenced in that way. I'll admit it—I was naive.

I often had to linotype little stories about inconsequential goings-on in the community. They would come in from service clubs or women's groups, written in longhand on little pieces of paper: "Last night, the Daughters of Rebecca hosted a party and voted to give

$25 to the Community Chest," or "The Daughters of
the American Revolution gave $5 toward So-and-So's
funeral expenses." A lot of this stuff was going into
the paper every day. It suddenly occurred to me that
my own local church congregation was participating
much more significantly in community service activities, and we weren't getting any of it into the paper.
And why not? Just because nobody took the trouble to
do it. That gave me the vision of what public relations
could do for my church. My experience on the *Ketchikan Chronicle* put the whole idea of public relations
in my mind.

The idea may have been in Murray's mind, but he kept
it in the back for a while. He returned to Decatur, Illinois, in
midsummer and married Virginia Hudgins on August 4,
1946. After a honeymoon in Chicago, the couple headed
to Southern California where Milton intended to finish his
degree at La Sierra College in Riverside, another Adventist
campus. Everything was coming together well. Milton was
happily married. He had seen the world—or at least some of
it. Southern California suited him, and he was eager to tackle
school again. The GI Bill and inexpensive housing solved
any serious financial worries, and he landed a part-time job
as a linotype operator on the *Riverside Press*.

In good mission-oriented style, Milton decided on the
premed course. His experience as a surgery scrub nurse in the
army had convinced him that he had what it took to be a
doctor. He had the interest and he had some solid, hands-on
experience in hospital wards. The one important thing he
lacked was grades, and it quickly became clear that he wasn't
going to get them.

Throughout my first year back in school I was a real
trooper with the books. In spare moments when I was
at the newspaper, with nothing to type, I'd pull out
my notebooks and study chemistry or biology. The
guys in the shop took to calling me "Doc." But I

discovered very quickly that everybody and his brother at La Sierra was taking premed and there were a lot of brains around there. We were all essentially competing against each other to get into the church's medical school at the College of Medical Evangelists [CME] twenty miles up the road in Loma Linda. And I was up against the kind of people who got into a real tizzy if they got an A-. Well, as you might guess, that really wasn't my speed. I was lucky to get a C+ or a B.

Toward the end of my first year at La Sierra (I spent five years in college—two in Michigan and three at La Sierra), I saw what happened to some of the senior premed majors down at the post office. I was there on the day they anticipated letters from the medical school about their applications. Just by looking in the mailbox they knew if they were in. A fat letter meant acceptance and a thin one meant rejection. It was a sad thing to watch. The fellows with the thin letters were devastated. Some of them broke into tears right there in the post office. They had wives, families, or the expectations of their parents. Their professional dreams were blasted. What would they do now? Try to finish another college major? That meant at least another year of school. I began to realize I might not want to go through that nonsense.

The next fall, in biology, we had a test where we had to name the fifty-four bones of a frog. I got fifty-one out of fifty-four, better than 90 percent, and was pretty pleased with myself until I discovered that my significant achievement had earned me a D—repeat, D—on the test. That did it. I went home and told my wife that I was quitting premed. She wasn't happy, because she had liked the idea that I would be a physician. I had liked it too, but it just wasn't realistic. (Even today, my wife says: "Your hours are as bad as a doctor's, but you don't make the same money.") I think that most of my adult life has demonstrated that I'm not a quitter. But there comes a time when one must read the handwriting on the wall. I was going to be judged and found very wanting.

Fortunately, I made this discovery while there was time to make a graceful midcourse correction. I didn't want one of those crises at the post office. During my first year at La Sierra I had done a little writing for the school newspaper. And of course I knew linotyping and printing and had been in newspaper work in Anchorage and Ketchikan. I suppose that it was natural for me to begin to think about journalism. In the late 1940s, La Sierra didn't offer a major in journalism. The closest program they had was English, so halfway through my second year there, at the time of that milestone frog-bone test, I switched from premed to English and was able to take a few journalism-related writing courses in the English department.

By this time, Murray was editing the school paper, the *Criterion,* for the 1947–48 school year. The student association officers had tapped him for the job the previous spring. Student journalism was still in its innocent childhood in the 1940s, at least on Adventist campuses. The newspapers were viewed largely as a means of eliciting approval and support from the school's constituency—primarily parents and the clergy. Judged, perhaps unfairly, by the more jaundiced attitudes of today's student journalism, the papers of the era generally presented a rosy and approving picture of college life and rarely risked controversy.

Murray, sensitive to the public relations role of the paper, nevertheless aimed for serious journalism. That year the *Criterion* won the All-American Honor Rating both semesters from the Associated Collegiate Press. And if Murray, as editor, didn't view himself as a PR man for the college, he certainly functioned as a PR man for the paper, finding ways to give the paper a high profile on campus beyond what would normally be earned by its function. He hired a reporter each day to write the world, national, and La Sierra headlines on a blackboard set up in the middle of the campus, with clear credit to the *Criterion* as the sponsor of this valuable service. Drew Pearson, the nationally known newspaper columnist, hosted a Freedom Train across the United States, carrying documents from the National Archives. When the train made a two-day stop in the Riverside area, Murray promoted the event on campus. In return, he received some exclusive material from Pearson for the *Criterion,* impressing the students that someone as distinguished as Pearson would write for their small college paper.

By the spring of his senior year, Murray's vision of his professional emphasis was coming into clear focus. The army had developed his personality, taught him about the real world, and given him an innocent and matter-of-fact fearlessness about tackling problems that other more sophisticated people would find daunting. He wanted to write—to be an editor or correspondent. The army had given him wisdom in the ways of the world. His mother had given him language skills. And his father had given him the ability to linotype.

He sent out letters to the church's three major publishing houses in the United States, hoping that his linotyping skills would be an entering wedge into editorial work. Nothing came of it. He then sent letters to the presidents of the church's ten regional administrative units in the United States and Canada.

> Every one of them wrote back and essentially said, "I'm sure there's a place for you in the Lord's work, but it isn't here. I trust the Lord will help you find what He wants you to do."
>
> Meanwhile, my senior classmates were getting their acceptance letters to medical school or job offers. One friend had fourteen job opportunities, and she was a music and secretarial major. I had no offers and I was getting a little worried. Our son had been born in February. My wife and I had agreed that I should work for our church organization, but I was not so dedicated that I'd settle for doing just anything. I wanted something in my professional area.

The real problem was that the church had almost no concept of organized public relations. There
was one man at Adventist World Headquarters who
wrote news releases, but there was no broad concept
of public relations. In the late 1940s, none of the
church's colleges or hospitals had public relations offices. I was asking my organization for a job that essentially did not exist.

As a safety precaution, I lined up a full-time
linotype job with the *Riverside Press* with the understanding that they *might,* some time in the future,
work me into the editorial room. But I was at the end
of my rope; I had done everything I could. And then a
man walked up to me on campus one day and changed
everything.

The man was Bruce Halstead, a medical doctor and
researcher from CME in nearby Loma Linda. A few months
before, Halstead and a colleague had been allowed to organize
a School of Tropical and Preventive Medicine within the medical college. They were primarily commissioned to conduct
research and publish their findings, thereby helping to satisfy
the concerns of the accrediting association, which was singu-
larly unimpressed with the faculty publication record at the
medical school.

Halstead wanted a public relations man on board to
put the new unit in the public eye and make it easier for the
school to attract funding for research. Institutional policy
required him to hire a church member and he had almost no
budget. This meant that he was looking for an entry-level
worker. No Adventist college offered a major in public relations or journalism at the time, so Halstead was limited to
graduates who had some related experience, such as newspaper work. Four decades later, Halstead, now director of the
World Life Research Foundation, remembers: "I shopped
around, and started to spread the word over at the La Sierra
campus. I asked people: 'Is there anybody here who is dy-
namic, is a good salesman, and can get along with people?' A

reply came back in a few days. There was a fellow on campus named Milton Murray, who was a real activist in student affairs. Everybody I talked to singled out Murray. So I went over there one Sunday morning to track him down."

Murray remembers the occasion distinctly.

That morning I was meeting with the class officers and the college business manager on the front lawn of the campus. We were deciding on a spot where we would place the new college sign my class was presenting to the school as a gift. I was treasurer of the class. As we stood there, a tall gentleman walked up to our group and said, "Which one of you is Milton Murray? I want to talk to him." When I identified myself, he said, "I'm Dr. Halstead from Loma Linda, and I'm here to find out whether you'd be interested in talking to us about a job as a PR person for the School of Tropical and Preventive Medicine."

Halstead took an immediate liking to Murray and was additionally impressed that Murray was fluently bilingual. A large portion of Halstead's research and study tours would be conducted in Spanish-speaking countries. Murray's language facility would be a great asset.

As far as Halstead and his colleague Harold Mozar were concerned, Murray had the job. But one more critical step remained before the matter was settled. On an appointed day in May, Murray showed up on the Loma Linda campus for the interview that really counted. And he knew it would be tough: "The administration at Loma Linda didn't really know what PR was, and they were sure they didn't need it. At that time, CME was the largest medical school west of the Mississippi and there was a certain self-confidence that went along with size. They thought that everyone—the medical profession and the public—knew all about the college. What more, of any value, could be done by a public relations office? Why should they spend their money on such a worthless venture?"

In reality, according to Halstead, the medical profession knew very little about CME and the public knew even less. CME's weak research and publishing record kept its name out of professional journals. "I think that CME's faculty were widely respected as medical practitioners," Halstead says. "But as a school contributing to the world of scientific research at that time, it was a zero." Harold Shryock, then dean of the medical school, affirms Halstead's evaluation. "There was no research going on, and those administrators who really knew what was going on understood that the kind of work Mozar and Halstead could do would provide an easier channel for credible, high-profile publications."

According to Shryock, the administration's knowledge of the situation did not always carry much weight with the board, which had no vision for what a PR program could do, especially when there didn't seem to be any money for a new position.

As far as CME's community interest and desire for local goodwill was concerned, Murray later found the medical school to be so preoccupied with its Great Commission to evangelize the remote corners of the earth that it ignored its immediate neighbors down the street. People in neighboring towns hardly knew it was there, in spite of its claim to be the largest medical school west of the Mississippi. Neither the board nor the administration seemed to understand or care about this discrepancy.

Such was the setting of Murray's memorable job interview.

Mozar and Halstead took me into a large laboratory room and sat me on a lab stool—it felt like a dunce stool—in front of about a dozen skeptical men: the chairman of the board of trustees, the college president, the academic dean, the assistant dean, the business manager, the hospital administrator, the personnel director, the dean of the clinical program in Los Angeles, the dean of students, and several others. After they finished their interrogation they dismissed me, went into session, and came up with a formal decision. They agreed to hire me for four months, with the understanding that for the first two months I would only work half-time. That was their bold move on behalf of public relations for CME.

Always an optimist, Murray ignored their pessimism. This was a godsend. He had a job, a chance to prove himself in this new and exciting work called public relations. It would be only five to six years before his vision of institutional advancement inevitably broadened to include organized fundraising and presented him with another and related set of challenges.

I ended up in a richly rewarding career in the same way that thousands of college students do today. I floundered around for a while, as so many do. But events (in my case, the army and some academic disappointments) stepped in and helped me to clarify my goals. As I matured into young adulthood, I finally took stock of my circumstances, saw the possibilities, and said, "This is it. I've got what it takes."

I had an innate self-confidence that left me unintimidated by others' apparent station or status, and that helped me to get along with people.

I had a set of values, instilled by my parents, that made me care for others.

I had a love for language, the printed word, and its process.

I had a vision of how society could be influenced for the better through creative communication.

I had a cause—in my case, my church organization and its institutions—that refined my vision and purpose and defined my area of potential contribution.

That is how I found my calling. Something similar, I believe, will help young adults today to hear the call of this rewarding career.

Milton Murray's first duty in June 1949 as a neophyte college PR man was to find himself a desk. Perhaps it was fitting that the best desk available was a beat-up army surplus item, tipped forlornly on its three good legs in a back storage room. Murray spent the remainder of his first day on the job down in the college maintenance shop, making the fourth leg.

4

Envisioning
the Future:
The Philanthropic
Fundraiser
as Leader

Effective leaders are generally characterized by such
qualities as: a strong drive for responsibility, vigor,
persistence, . . . ability to delegate, humor, . . . fairness, self-confidence, decisiveness, . . . capacity to
organize.

—*Fisher, 1984, p. 24*

Nearly thirty objects hang on the walls of Milton Murray's
office. Among them are the Harold J. Seymour Award from
AHP, the Outstanding Fund-Raising Executive of the Year
Award from NSFRE, diplomas for his status as a Fellow of
AHP and a Certified Fund-Raising Executive from NSFRE,
an honorary doctorate, two honored alumni citations and a
general tribute of thanks from four Adventist colleges and
universities, a citation from the American Protestant Health
Association, and a plaque commemorating the establishment
of the Milton Murray Foundation for Philanthropy.

Other items include a matted and framed letter from
Barbara Bush, thanking Milton for sending her one of his
philanthropy calendars; a similarly dressed presidential proc-

lamation signed by Barbara's husband, certifying that Murray was a guest of the president at the dedication of the Camp David Chapel; and a shiny black glass plaque etched in silver, with a poem titled "A Tribute to Milton," presented to him by an admiring protégé. On the wall behind the door in the small office hangs a glassed display of sixty U.S. postage stamps honoring different philanthropic endeavors. Murray designed the collage himself.

Directly facing Murray's desk on the front wall is a richly framed, inexpensive reprint of Norman Rockwell's whimsical self-portrait, a study of the bespectacled illustrator craning to observe himself in a mirror beside his easel while applying a brush to the canvas. Yet even this rare esthetic touch in Murray's office is amended for utilitarian use. In a wide margin at the bottom of the print, a caption reads: "Every job is a self-portrait of the person who did it."

The quotation is significant, not only for what it says about Murray's philosophy of work, but as evidence of one of Murray's hobbies: he collects inspirational quotations. One last item, another quotation, adorns a wall of the office. It is mounted immediately to his right, within arm's reach as he sits at his desk, or directly in front of him at eye level when he uses his typewriter. Of all the items on his walls it is the plainest—a five-by-seven-inch sheet of rough-textured beige paper, under glass in a simple brown wood frame, upon which appears, in thick, dark brown type, another of Murray's favorite quotations, this one attributed to Niccolo Machiavelli:

There is nothing more difficult to carry out, nor more doubtful of success, nor more dangerous to handle, than to initiate a new order of things.

For the reformer has enemies in all who profit by the old order, and only lukewarm defenders in all those who would profit by the new order.

This lukewarmness arises partly from fear of their adversaries who have the law in their favor; and partly from the incredulity of mankind, who do not truly believe in anything new until they have had actual experience of it.

For Murray, the quotation is not so much a nugget of inspiration as an artful recitation of reality. For virtually all of his professional life he has known the doubts and the dangers of initiating new orders, of leading the way by leading the leaders. His fascination with leadership has pioneered new programs, produced important publications, advanced his professional organizations, and inspired or mentored dozens of practitioners in the generation to come.

Milton Murray's education in leadership began during his work at CME, where his entire eleven-year tenure became a relentless struggle to establish an institutional public relations program for an administration that thought it largely unnecessary. There, leadership became his passion. He thought about it. He read about it. He wrote about it. He collected quotations about it. And he practiced it. Convinced early on that he would never be a "leader" as it is commonly understood by job title or public acclaim, he found his niche and his satisfaction from making things happen *through* recognized leaders, or in spite of them. Three experiences at Loma Linda taught him that new orders may be initiated, and real leadership effected, by agitation, by influence, and by innocent subterfuge.

In 1953 Murray discovered that CME was ripe for an important anniversary celebration, but no one seemed to understand. Adventists had bought property and opened a sanitarium and nursing school in Loma Linda in 1905, with the specific purpose of establishing a medical education center. The medical school, chartered in 1909, quickly became the focus of attention and institutional identity, overshadowing the nursing school and the hospital, built in Los Angeles in 1913, that served as its clinical facility.

When Murray pointed out that 1955 ought to be observed as the fiftieth anniversary of CME, he had a hard sell.

I went to some key members of the administration and suggested that we should do something in 1955. I was told, firmly, that I was wrong, because the School of Medicine wasn't chartered until 1909; therefore, CME's fiftieth anniversary wouldn't be observed until 1959. Even the school seal that some administrator had commissioned in years past said 1909. According to the thinking of the time, dominated primarily by the physicians, CME was a medical school, "and don't you forget it. Medicine is the only thing that counts." I argued that although it was true that medicine was the core, CME was more than just the medical school. A nursing school, a dietetics program, and two major hospitals, all integral parts of CME, were making an important contribution to the community and to the mission of the institution. Any organization that's trying to understand its history and to establish its identity looks to the earliest legitimate date when things began to roll. In the case of CME, this occurred when the church bought the property in 1905, opened a sanitarium, and started a nursing school, all with the express purpose of establishing a health education center. That was the beginning of the institution. Other developments, including the chartering of the medical school four years later, were just that—developments. If an institution is established in 1990 and reorganized in 2020, you won't forget the first thirty years and say you were founded in 2020; you say that you were founded in 1990.

This was the logic I used on the administration. It was difficult for some people to accept because it implied that the medical school wasn't the only thing that mattered. Fortunately, a few others who were more broadminded and visionary about Loma Linda's mission helped change the thinking. And of course I had the School of Nursing fighting for the idea.

When the administrators finally became convinced that 1955 and not 1959 should be observed as CME's fiftieth anniversary, they asked me how much the celebration would cost. I suggested $50,000—$1,000 a year for each year the school had been in existence. It had a nice ring to it. When, as I predicted, the administrators were scandalized by that figure, I said, "Of course, we can engineer something for $50. But that's all you'll get—$50 worth. And I think the fiftieth anniversary deserves more than $50."

They suggested that I come back to the committee with a budget somewhere between those two figures. I took that to mean $25,000. So I went around to the deans of the schools and directors of departments and got them excited about special events, such as luncheons, banquets, and concerts, that they could host for their areas that would contribute meaningfully to the anniversary celebration. I also outlined some major schoolwide events. I put these all together on one list with dollar estimates attached that totaled an overall budget of $25,000. This still shocked the committee members and they told me to scale down even further.

That was the easy part. I simply went back to the deans and department directors and said, "You know, a few weeks ago I talked with you about having that luncheon for your department in connection with the fiftieth anniversary. I am sorry, but I've been told to reduce the budget, so we have to cut out that luncheon." But by this time those deans and directors were so excited about their events that they reinstituted them in their own budgets. I went back to the committee with a $15,000 budget, having cut out of the budget several events that were now going to happen anyway. I couldn't have been happier. As the prime agitator behind the fiftieth anniversary celebration, I knew that my institution was going to have a successful event, and yet my neck wouldn't be on the block for a lot of the cost. It was a PR man's dream.

Murray's leadership of the fiftieth anniversary celebration produced a year-long program of festivities, including a

speech by Vice President Richard Nixon, the inauguration of
the School of Dentistry building, a collegewide consecration
service, and a joint picnic involving students and staff from
the clinical departments in Los Angeles and the academic
operation in Loma Linda. The anniversary inspired a new
school motto, "To Make Man Whole," which is still used to
this day, and provided universal recognition that the school
now called Loma Linda University was established in 1905
and not 1909. They changed the school seal.

Murray learned about two other kinds of leadership at
Loma Linda, which were more to his liking because they
kept him out of the public eye and yet helped him to "initiate
a new order of things." In the early 1950s, CME faced a difficult identity problem. Organized as one institution, it con-
sisted of two distinct and even distant operations. The basic
science programs for the School of Medicine were located in
Loma Linda. The clinical training programs took place sixty-
five miles away at White Memorial Hospital in downtown
Los Angeles. The School of Nursing was forming a collegiate
program out of two hospital programs. Through the years,
separate identities had developed and it was not easy for
employees, firmly attached to one operation or the other, to
grasp the whole picture of what the institution was trying to
accomplish as a unit.

Each week Murray joined other administrators in working two days in Los Angeles. He saw the identity problem
and concluded that terminology was at least part of the cause.
Up to that point, it was customary for the institution to refer
to CME's Loma Linda "division" and Los Angeles "division." In Murray's mind, the term connoted separateness and
independence, the very thing he, as the public relations officer, was working against.

> I was trying to promote unity of understanding, of
> mission, of purpose, and here we were using the term
> "division" to describe our integral parts. It didn't
> make sense to me. So one day I went to an appropriate
> committee and said that we needed to have "cam-

puses" instead of "divisions," to fit the pattern of higher education.

I got nowhere. The committee said it wouldn't work. They said people couldn't think of a hospital as a campus. They said the stationery, for years, had said "division." They said the cost to change would be prohibitive. Blah, blah, blah.

Agitation and persuasion had failed, so I decided to use the power of my position—limited though it was—to influence. When I got back to my office I called in my editor of campus publications and said, "We will no longer use the word 'division.' We will say 'the Loma Linda campus,' and 'the Los Angeles campus.' " So that is what we did, quietly and consistently, in all our publications, news releases, and public presentations. Within two years I saw the stationery begin to change. That gave me a certain degree of confidence that I could change things by influence even when I had failed to persuade my colleagues and superiors. As long as I wasn't doing anything immoral, I figured that was the way to go about it. I could effect change—that is, lead—without always needing the sanction of the powers that be. Sometimes, and I stress *sometimes,* you're better off just going ahead and doing something. If the people in the big office don't like it, they can call you in and tell you so. And then you can say, "I'm sorry."

Murray's agitation for CME's fiftieth anniversary had forced him to learn something about the school's history. In the process he realized that there was no organized plan for preserving that history. The school had recently built a new library and there was a small area in the new building that Murray and others thought would be ideal for a historical records office. The administration maintained that there was no budget to staff such an office. Murray recalls saying, "This is a job for a librarian and not me, but if you don't do something, I'll start keeping a file in my office."

At the same time, Murray had been lobbying to add another person to the public relations staff. When the administration approved his staffing request, Murray promptly split the full-time budget with the library to hire a half-time archivist. Today, the Heritage Room at Loma Linda University is one of the most important archives of Seventh-day Adventist history anywhere. Murray avers that his actions were honest. He sincerely needed a full-time person on his staff. Only after the budget was granted did he realize that he probably could muddle through with a half-time staffer for the sake of establishing an archive.

These were small matters, specific and localized illustrations of how Murray, as a young professional, learned the ropes of leadership by agitation, influence, or (apparent) subterfuge. But he was leading in large-scale ways as well, on projects that required a skillful combination of all three techniques. Shortly after the conclusion of the highly successful fiftieth anniversary celebration, Murray attended an administrative committee meeting where the subject of the anniversary came up. He recalls that the members of the committee seemed to be in a good mood and began remarking on their delight that the year-long festivities had been a great success, had stayed within budget, had boosted morale, and had unified the institution. Because of his high-profile involvement with the celebration, much of the praise was directed toward Murray.

When they were through talking, I said, "I'm very happy you all liked what happened. I enjoyed it too, and we had a lot of fun. Yes, it was very good for the institution, but we made a great error of omission." I let that hang in the air for a moment and they began to mumble, "What's he talking about? What didn't we do? What happened?" I said, "If this institution had really been on the ball, we would have had another committee working on fundraising to capitalize on the anniversary. We've done nothing about fundraising and have missed a great opportunity."

Murray's speech, which for the moment may have seemed depressing, accomplished its purpose. The administration, which to that point had been uninterested in pursuing outside fundraising, now caught Murray's vision. As he recalls the incident, the administrators even began to put him on the defensive, asking why he hadn't done more about fundraising. Secretly, he was delighted with their accusing tone and his answer was calculated to protect himself while keeping them disturbed and the momentum going. He said that he had been forced to work so hard selling the idea of the anniversary in the first place, and then planning and running the activities, that he simply hadn't had the time to initiate any fundraising. Satisfied for the moment, the now-agitated administrators weren't through with the subject. The next day the business manager called Murray and told him he had been appointed director of development, the responsibilities to be added to his present job as coordinator of public relations.

It was January of 1956 and Murray was ready, even though he had never raised a dime. For several years he had been attending meetings of ACPRA and the American Alumni Council (AAC), the forerunners of CASE. He had learned what was being done in fundraising at the University of Chicago, Stanford, and other large schools, which by the 1950s had developed some impressive programs. He was eager to apply to his own institution the principles he had learned at professional conferences. At the same time, and despite the apparent momentary enthusiasm for development exhibited by a few administrators, he knew he would face the same inherent prejudice he had struggled against in developing a public relations program. In addition, CME had had one unfortunate episode with fundraising in the past that had confirmed many leaders in their prejudice. Murray recalls:

In the mid 1940s, the Los Angeles campus (White Memorial Hospital) brought in a fundraising firm. They took a survey of the hospital and the Los Angeles community and told the administration: "You people are terrific! You've got a great story to tell! We will raise a million dollars for you." At the end of six months they had charged fees of $75,000 and had raised $80,000. They gave up and said, "Look, you are great people, but you don't have any friends in the community. You don't have any real leaders who know how a community works." And, of course, it was true. Unfortunately, that soured CME administrators and trustees on the possibilities of philanthropy. For the next ten years they dismissed the potential of fundraising instead of going out, making friends, and changing the conditions that had caused those poor results.

These were the conditions Murray faced in 1956, when his impromptu speech in a committee meeting earned him some extra words in his job title. At that time the CME alumni association, controlled primarily by loyal but strong-willed physicians, was largely autonomous in its operations. Murray had no authority to meddle in alumni fundraising, which, in other contexts, might have been the logical place to start. He realized that before Loma Linda could raise any serious money for development, it had to have a long-range plan spelling out what it wished to accomplish. No such plan existed, so early in 1956 Murray, with strong support from the top administration, began organizing a development conference to establish plans and to acquaint the institution with possible ways to achieve them.

Between June 1 and the end of September, four committees met to determine the broad outlines of the institution's financial needs for the next decade in the areas of teaching, physical plant, student policies and welfare, and extension of community services. Each committee prepared a written report. The reports, outlining tentative financial expansion needs totaling $23 million in the next decade, were gathered in a single document and distributed to participants in order to brief them in advance of the conference. The introduction to the document made it clear that the committees' reports were provided only as source material for discussion at the conference and were not binding. It stated: "The matter of *when* these elements may develop and *how* any goals are to be reached is something to be considered by trustees and administrators *after* (1) the recommendations of the September 23 Conference are reviewed by the College; (2) a Second Development Conference is held with wider representation of CME publics; and (3) trustees have given formal approval to a plan for growth."

From the start, it was an ambitious undertaking, and the action plan, including the announcement of a second conference before the first one had even met, sent signals that the school was becoming serious about long-range planning, with the implication that it would turn its attention to fundraising.

Murray was encouraged. This was progress. At last, CME was ready to come out of its shell and make friends in the real world. Or so it seemed.

Murray had a high profile in the development conferences. He was secretary of the trustee committee on development, one of the sponsors of the conference; chairman of the committee on the extension of community services; and chairman of the subcommittee that planned the conference.

Murray designed the conference for eighty participants: eight students, twenty alumni, forty faculty members, and twelve administrators, all of whom, according to the briefing document, represented "a group of people who are keenly interested in CME."

The one-day program focused mainly on group sessions in which conference participants, divided into groups by areas of expertise, reacted to the committee reports and later summarized those reactions in a report in the plenary session. A resolution and recommendations committee submitted actions for the conference to vote on during the last hour of the day. In Murray's view, the program was a great success.

By the time the second development conference met a year later, Murray could see ominous signs that his dream was losing steam. The institution had become preoccupied with a protracted political struggle over whether to combine all academic and clinical operations on a single campus in Loma Linda. That controversy made the plans of the two development conferences moot. At the same time, it became clear to Murray that CME, and the church at large, still did not understand what professional fundraising was all about. Organizing volunteers and making friends in the "secular" world were foreign concepts, and most Adventists did not understand that those activities had to take place before anything could be accomplished. Instead, church leaders and CME administrators tended to look for quick, impressive results without doing their homework. When Murray advocated the unglamorous but tried-and-true way, they couldn't comprehend what he was talking about, or they wrote him off as a nice young man who had a few good ideas along with a lot of irrelevant interests.

From his earliest days as a public relations officer, Murray nurtured those "irrelevant interests" by taking a decidedly active interest in his own professional development. Not by nature a formal scholar, he still decided to use some of the college credits he had left over from the GI Bill. Typical of his general belief that there is always something to be learned nearby, he registered for a summer school class in college relations, taught by Gil Brown, the director of public relations at the University of Redlands. Murray recalls the class.

There were three of us in the class: the student sportswriter from Brown's own department, a housewife who needed a few elective hours during the summer, and me. That's when I really began to see what college public relations could be. Brown introduced me to ACPRA, a forerunner of CASE. If I had waited for someone in the Adventist educational system to alert me to what was going on in the real world of college public relations, I'd still be back at Loma Linda writing news releases about the School of Tropical and Preventive Medicine. Gil Brown's class opened my eyes to what could be done and what was being done in higher education in those days. He gave me a perspective I couldn't have gotten in any other way.

That perspective provided Murray with all the incentive he needed to plunge into professional activities. He joined ACPRA and AAC and became editor of ACPRA's regional newsletter. He served a term as program director and then became district director, which earned him a position on the ACPRA board. He and Bob Pierce, an AAC member from Stanford University, staged the first regional conference anywhere in the country that was jointly sponsored by AAC and ACPRA. Murray and Pierce were sensitive to the rivalry between the competing organizations, but neither of them tried to outrank the other. Murray says, "I like to think that the joint regional conference was a milestone for the two organizations and perhaps one of many small stepping-stones leading to their eventual merger as CASE."

By the late 1950s, Murray was, as he says, "beginning to become somebody" in ACPRA. Unfortunately, his professional leadership was beginning to bloom at the very time when his occupational situation would make that professional leadership impossible. Murray became discouraged at Loma Linda. He felt that he had failed to convince the board and the administration of the possibilities of philanthropic support. It became clear to him that until someone within the organization made a success in philanthropy outside the church institutions, the leadership would never take philanthropy seriously.

I had used every tactic I knew to show them the value of making friends in the community, and the resulting opportunities for raising money. Yet even after nine or ten years with an active PR program, we were still as isolated as we could be and still be on the map. I felt that I was failing. Occasionally I'd get an encouraging word from one or two key board members or an administrator, just enough to keep me hanging on a

while longer. But in the long run, it was clear that
nothing was happening. The development conferences
had been good while they lasted, but the institution
became distracted. This wasn't just a CME problem.
It was a church problem, because the CME board was
composed of the top leadership of the church. If I was
going to be any good in proving my case, I'd have to
do it outside the church first, and then they'd see the
light—maybe!

Murray left Loma Linda and took a job with the G. A.
Brakeley Company. His experience there greatly enriched and
matured his expertise as a fundraiser. But it also cost him
dearly in professional leadership status. As a consultant in a
for-profit fundraising firm, Murray became ineligible to hold
offices in ACPRA. In a roundabout way, he still blames this
on CME and counts it his greatest professional disappointment. He loved his profession and he wanted to serve it by
being active in its societies. The combination of his loyalty
to, and long-term goals for, his church organization and a
lack of vision on the part of his institution and its leadership
prompted him to leave Loma Linda, an action that sacrificed
most of his rapidly developing professional influence.

After three years with Brakeley, Murray spent three more
years establishing a development office at the Autonomous
University of Guadalajara, sponsored by the Ford Foundation.
Theoretically, this post would have allowed him to resume his
association with the newly formed CASE. But higher education in Mexico was very different from how it was in the
United States, and Murray felt his distance from the mainstream, so he found other ways to contribute to his profession.
Mexico became a kind of professional mission field.

Guadalajara was a great experience for me because
it made me get down to the hard fundamentals of
what this business was about and why we were
doing it. To go through another language, you
must cut away all the fat in your philosophy and

get to the bare-bones purposes of your program. It was excellent discipline.

You could talk yourself hoarse about direct mail and alumni affairs. But the reality was that the mail service was not dependable and the university had hardly any concept of what "alumni" are, let alone having any alumni records. So I had to start from the very bottom by explaining why alumni are important to the institution and why there should be alumni records. I had to help them formulate a program that would not begin to be productive for at least a year, or more likely two or three years. I couldn't talk about alumni chapters or class agents. It was almost like trying to explain the color green to someone who has been blind from birth.

In this setting, away from the associations of his colleagues in U.S. higher education, Murray was nevertheless getting some professional fulfillment just by teaching the nationals in his office about fundraising. Language was the biggest problem. Although Murray was fluent in Spanish, his associates didn't read English. Since all professional advancement literature, including CASE's publication *Currents,* came from the United States, this resource was largely inaccessible to his colleagues. At the weekly staff meeting, Murray introduced some article on a relevant topic and translated it informally for the benefit of the staff. In 1966, he obtained a copy of the first edition of Harold Seymour's *Designs for Fund-Raising* (Seymour, 2nd ed., 1988) and followed the same routine week by week, chapter by chapter, until his associates had heard the whole book.

The weekly Seymour readings gave Murray another opportunity to advance his profession. He decided to arrange for the publication of Seymour's book in Spanish. At this time, he was leaving his work in Mexico and setting up shop in Dayton, Ohio, as a general consultant to Adventist schools and hospitals in the eastern United States. He knew little of the publishing business, particularly outside the United States.

He had heard that the U.S. State Department sometimes helped to produce translations of important books. Seymour's book was, and still is, regarded by many as the bible of the fundraising profession. In Murray's thinking, how better could the State Department contribute to the development of Third World countries than by encouraging the growth of professional philanthropy? His contact in the U.S. embassy in Mexico City was slow to see the importance of Seymour's book. Murray recalls that the man thought the book much too specialized and technical to be of interest to the market the State Department was developing.

> The official said that he would have to have requests, through the U.S. embassies in Central and South America, totaling one thousand books before he would be interested. From my office in Dayton I started writing letters to universities, hospitals, social service agencies, Red Cross offices, and other nonprofit, humanitarian entities of all kinds throughout Latin America. I told them that the translation was in the works and explained how it would benefit their work and the cause of philanthropy in general. I asked them to write to the U.S. embassies in their countries and urge those embassies, in turn, to write to the U.S. embassy in Mexico, which would coordinate the Spanish translation. It was an enormous task to make all those contacts and our success depended on everyone up the line catching the vision and following through. I suppose that I contacted more than two hundred organizations.
>
> One day, when I was in Mexico City, I stopped in to see my contact at the embassy. He said, "Murray, we've only got seven hundred orders for your book. But you are so persistent that we're going to do it."

Persuading the State Department to fund the project was one thing. Finding a publisher was another. At the time, Murray was spending a lot of time away from his Dayton, Ohio, office, consulting for several institutions in Mexico and Colombia. He queried a major publishing house in Mexico and was rejected. He then approached another firm in Colombia and was turned down, but he had some leverage. He says, "The chairman of the board of that Colombian publishing house also was the chairman of the board of the university foundation I was working for. So I went to the big man himself and said, 'Hey, your company won't consider printing a book on philanthropy. What's going on here? I thought we wanted to nurture philanthropy here in Latin America.' "

Within a month he heard from the Colombian firm that they would do the book. By that time, the house in Mexico had changed its mind, too. Murray chose the Mexican publisher because it was more convenient to his travels.

The State Department contracted the translation with a couple in France and Murray edited it, adjusting some of the technical terminology. He saw the first fruits of his labor come off the press in 1970, three years after he started the project. Murray says that he doesn't have a reliable way of gauging the impact of the book, but his latest understanding is that nearly four thousand copies are in circulation in Latin America and that the edition went through a second printing. To his knowledge, the translation of Seymour's book is the only major text on fundraising in the Spanish-speaking world.

Murray's dogged leadership on this project added luster to his standing in professional fundraising circles. He credits the translation with providing the key factor in his selection as the 1980 recipient of the Harold J. Seymour Award from AHP.

Publishing became a private Murray hobby. In 1981, with two colleagues, Viveca Black and Sheree Parris Nudd, Murray produced a thirty-two-page booklet titled *Accent on Philanthropy,* containing more than 250 eloquent quotations related to humanitarian concerns. In the fall of that year, Murray placed notices in CASE's *Currents,* the *Fund Raising Institute Bulletin,* the *Ragan Report,* the *Fund Raising Management Newsletter,* and similar publications, advertising free single copies. Within a few months he had received more than 200 requests from schools, hospitals, foundations, cultural organizations, and humanitarian agencies. Because the copies were giveaways, the advertising cost him nothing. However, each booklet that went out carried information on how the reader could purchase additional copies to give away to friends and donors. Within a year, more than 5,000 copies had been sold. Free copies of a second volume, *Accent on Philanthropy II*, were similarly advertised in late 1982 and early 1983. This time Murray received more than 400 requests and distributed more than 15,000 copies.

Success breeds success, and Murray's appetite for publishing had been thoroughly whetted. A more ambitious project, *Accent on Recognition*, appeared in 1985. The seventy-two-page booklet highlighted techniques for expressing thanks and giving appropriate and meaningful recognition to donors. By 1990, more than 14,500 copies were in print. A book, *Accent on Humor*, highlighted the lighter side of philanthropy and sold more than 10,000 copies in two years. Even as he introduced these publications, Murray and his associates were working on the most significant publishing enterprise of his career.

Each one claims that the other first articulated the idea, but Milton Murray and Sheree Parris Nudd together were the minds behind the "Giving Is Caring" page-a-day philanthropy calendar. Sheree Parris Nudd has been a Murray admirer and protégé since her first job out of college in 1976. Now vice president of Shady Grove Adventist Hospital in Maryland, she began her career at Huguley Memorial Hospital in Fort Worth, Texas, at the same time that Murray was wrapping up the campaign that built the 150-bed facility. A neophyte fundraiser who was beginning to build a highly successful program of her own at Huguley, she snagged Murray as her mentor, professional adviser, and confidant.

In 1981, Nudd and Murray collaborated on the first edition of *Accent on Philanthropy* out of a shared predilection for inspirational quotations. Nudd's Christmas gift to Murray in 1984 was the spark of their new idea. The gift was a page-a-day calendar, published by Workman Publishing Company in New York, with, as Nudd describes it, "quotations on generic topics." As Murray was thanking her, one of them thought of asking Workman to publish a calendar with quotes about philanthropy.

Murray found a phone number for Workman Publishing Company.

> I called and told the receptionist that I wanted to talk to the person in charge of the company. I suppose a lot of other people would have written a letter, but through the years I've gotten used to going right to the top with the telephone and it's worked out well for me. The receptionist said, "You mean Peter Workman?" and I said, "If that's who he is." She put me through, and I told him, without going into detail, that I wanted to talk to him about a calendar for the nonprofit world. He gave me an appointment.
>
> A few weeks later I was in his office in New York. I showed him our latest book on philanthropy quotations and said that there might be some merit in putting out a page-a-day calendar about love, charity, giving, compassion, kindness, wealth, poverty, service, gratitude, and other topics that relate to the caring aspect of human nature.
>
> He listened thoughtfully and then said, "It won't sell."
>
> "Why not?"
>
> "Because it doesn't appeal to people in a way that would make them want to buy it. I sell calendars and books that appeal to people's ego and drive to succeed, or their passion for entertainment. You're trying to get them to spend money for something that tells them to be unselfish and to think about the other guy. That doesn't work."
>
> I got a little preachy. "Isn't that a rather sad commentary about American society?"

"Sure it is," Workman replied. "But that's the way it is."

"Well, how about just printing the calendars for me? I'll sell them."

Workman said that he would, and he gave me a good price, but it required a purchase of 10,000 calendars. How was I going to sell 10,000 calendars? I was confident that it was a good idea, but it had some problems, too.

I knew that nonprofit organizations would have a use for this product because the price range—four or five dollars—was perfect. Organizations need something to give to volunteers and modest donors. It's tough to find anything under the six- to ten-dollar range, and on the upper end of that you are pricing yourself out. Even now, I wish there was a really meaningful product that could sell for two or three dollars, but today you won't get much for that beyond a glorified bookmark.

This calendar represented our profession in a meaningful way and yet had potential use to the recipient. Unfortunately, it was a *calendar*. There are hundreds, maybe thousands, of calendars on the market. Just go to Waldenbooks or B. Dalton or Crown between October and December and you'll see what I mean. Everybody has calendars. Mine was going to be a tough sell. In the final analysis, I knew that the calendar wasn't as great an idea as I would have liked, but it did have some potential and it raised the profile of philanthropy. I thought it was worth a try.

Murray hired a summer student intern to begin editing the manuscript by collecting quotations to add to the 150 to 200 that Murray and Nudd had already published in the *Accent* series. Meanwhile, Murray wrote to major organizations that promoted philanthropy, including NSFRE, AHP, CASE, the Association of Governing Boards, and INDEPENDENT SECTOR.

I gave them all the reasons why this was a great idea and why they ought to order some calendars, sight unseen, to promote and distribute through their organizations. I mentioned that I had to order 10,000 to get a good price. They all wrote back and said, "This is a great idea. We'll be happy to tell others about it. Unfortunately, we can't order any calendars right now." The only exception was CASE. Virginia Carter Smith said that CASE would buy 4,000. With that order in my pocket, I gambled that I could sell 2,500 to Adventist hospitals and colleges. That 6,500 was all I needed to redeem my investment. Even if I pushed the last 3,500 over a cliff with a bulldozer, I still wouldn't lose any money—except for the cost of renting the bulldozer!

Murray went to the treasury department of Adventist World Headquarters with a requisition for $33,000 to print 10,000 calendars. After grilling Murray for assurances that the cost would be recouped, the treasurers approved the purchase order.

Murray sold the 10,000 calendars within a few weeks and saw the clear prospect of selling at least that many more. He returned to the church treasurers, by now beginning to catch Murray's vision, with a requisition for 12,000 more calendars. This time he had no advance orders, so he persuaded a donor friend to help cover the loss if the second printing did not sell. He did manage to sell the second printing, but sometimes it was slow going. Murray and his staff frequently found themselves hauling boxes of calendars to conventions and selling them in twos and threes. But the base had been built, and Murray knew whom to thank. He says, "The idea would never have gotten off the ground if Virginia Carter Smith and CASE had not had the courage to support me that first year. With their help and the resulting momentum of that initial order, the calendar began to develop a following and a modest market in advancement offices all across the country. That was how the whole enterprise started." After that first year, the market expanded quickly throughout the nonprofit sector. The 1992 edition sold 60,000 copies, with 40,000 ordered before Workman even printed the calendars.

Although Murray had sold 2,500 calendars to Adventist hospitals and colleges in the first year for distribution as "thank-yous" to their donors, he was disappointed that more entities in his church organization were not participating. He persuaded his major donor friends to pledge three years of seed money to help the church promote philanthropy in the general society by giving calendars to all state legislators across the country. The tactic worked. When the donors' three-year pledge was fulfilled, the church leaders, who by then realized the public relations potential of the enterprise, picked up the entire cost. Murray also worked with NSFRE to persuade the Lilly Foundation to give the calendars to all U.S. representatives and senators, and the Gannett Foundation sent them to the CEOs of Fortune 500 companies. By early 1992, Murray had distributed more than 250,000 copies of his philanthropy calendar to business and political leaders, volunteers, and donors across the nation.

Murray insists that he got into the calendar business only because he wanted to do something to raise the profile of philanthropy in American society. He had no intention of making money, even though it was important that the operation break even. The Adventist leadership was perfectly willing to support the venture if it wouldn't cost any money. Between the small margin on sales and the financial help of his key donors, Murray soon built up a reserve fund of more than $100,000, from which he has made small but high-profile incentive grants back to organizations like CASE, NSFRE, AHP, the American Association of Fund-Raising Counsel Trust, and the National Philanthropy Day Committee to support other philanthropic programs.

This is the Murray brand of leadership. Find an idea that has merit and push it relentlessly and creatively until others see the light and move ahead on their own. The philanthropy calendar is a small model of some of the unusual ways in which Murray has provided leadership, in his own sphere, for the entire philanthropic profession.

Murray gravitates toward leadership activities in whatever setting he finds himself. When he left higher education advancement in 1961 to work for the G. A. Brakeley Company, he lost most of his professional contacts in ACPRA. When he moved to Guadalajara, his work, although it was back in the field of philanthropy for higher education, still kept him out of the mainstream of American educational advancement. In 1967, Murray accepted a position offered by the Adventist church to consult for institutions in the eastern states. For the next twelve years his professional work concentrated almost exclusively on health care. As a result, he instinctively involved himself with the National Association for Hospital Development, now the AHP.

At a meeting in 1980, Murray heard the association's leaders worrying about the sorry state of the education fund that was designed to promote professional development among its members.

I went to one of the association's leaders and said, "If you want to raise money from the members, I'll be happy to help." They asked if I wanted to chair the AHP Foundation. I said, "No, but I'll be happy to do the member campaign."

At the time, AHP was raising about $6,000 per year from the members for the educational fund. I thought we should raise that to $10,000. So I asked one of my major donor friends if he would give us $5,000 the following year if we raised $10,000 or more in the current year. We raised $12,000 and then, with similar subsequent challenges for four years, brought the total up to $30,000. With the habit of giving firmly developed among a significant portion of the membership, the annual fund, by 1991, had risen to $100,000.

I suppose that it was an unusual arrangement. The donor was an enterprising friend of mine who up to that point had not given to such a broad-based and generic cause. But I think he liked what I was doing enough that he was willing to contribute in a modest way to help the philanthropy profession across the board.

Murray involved this donor friend and others in a similar way from 1988 to 1990 to raise the NSFRE Every Member campaign's annual yield from $29,000 to more than $60,000.

For Murray, leadership means personal action rather than talk. He tells of attending a meeting several years ago in Washington, D.C., where an organized group of local church intelligentsia worried about college students of their denomination who attended universities in the city and had no relationship with a local congregation. The consensus of the meeting was to call upon the regional or national church headquarters to fund a coordinator who would identify these young, potentially wayward members and organize programs and social activities to keep them congregationally involved. Murray was touched by their well-meaning concern but was annoyed at the assumption that church headquarters should cough up the money with no commitment by the members, who undoubtedly were congratulating themselves for pointing out yet another problem "the establishment" should solve.

At the close of the meeting, Murray approached the discussion leader and asked, "How much money would be necessary to do what you are proposing?" The leader suggested $35,000. "Fine," said Murray. "You raise half of that, and I'll help you with the other half." The next day, Murray put the commitment in writing in a letter to the head of the organization. He never heard another word about it.

In 1986, Murray became a member of the National Philanthropy Day Committee, a group organized in 1983 by Douglas Freeman, a planned-giving attorney in Los Angeles, to give recognition to the role of philanthropy in American society. Murray joined on the condition that the committee adopt his campaign for a philanthropy stamp as part of the National Philanthropy Day agenda.

One day we were meeting in Washington, D.C., at the American Red Cross building. We realized that in order to accomplish anything we needed some money, and we set a starter goal of $30,000. We talked in that meeting for quite a while about how we were going to get the money, or even *if* we could. I started talking to myself: "Murray, you're not a big-time operator like some of the other people here. You're not a trustee of a university or a major organization. But at this moment, serving on this committee, you are something like a trustee, so you should act like one. For years you've been yelling about how trustees are supposed to lead or get out of the way. This is your moment. What are you going to do?"

Finally, I said, "Friends, I don't represent any major nonprofit organization from a leadership position. I don't have access to the funds that you do. But I have a small margin in my philanthropy calendar fund, and I will give $2,000 toward this goal."

They thought that was wonderful. When I told them I'd send the check within sixty days, that seemed to set the tone. The others followed my example and pledged $2,000 each. We essentially raised our goal at that meeting.

Murray has developed a philosophy of leadership, which he describes with clarity.

First, make changes in small steps. If you are "initiating a new order of things" for an organization from a middle-management position, you probably will be more successful if you break your idea down into small pieces and present them one at a time. Great human enterprises are nourished by great ideas, but committees or administrations generally can't handle them easily. It's just as Machiavelli said: those who benefit from, or are satisfied with, the old ways are betting on a sure thing, something they know, and will oppose you. Those who will benefit from your new idea will be more cautious, because they are taking a risk. Your supporters are shaky and your opponents are bold.

You must find an approach that doesn't threaten anyone, doesn't cost a lot of money, and doesn't cause an uproar in some other element of the organization. You must plan and strategize: How do I do this? Do I have to have approval? Do I need more support? Do I have access to the necessary money for the first step?

You must have patience. Achieving success may take you six weeks, six months, or six years. It shouldn't matter. If you "want it now," then middle-management leadership—that is, leading the leaders— is not the game for you.

Most of us are more content to criticize leadership than we are to knuckle down and *do* anything. We think we are making an outstanding contribution by calling a problem to everybody's attention.

When it comes to leadership in your profession, start by making the case for your work in your own institution. Sometimes it will be a hard sell. We cannot advance philanthropic fundraising in America without persuading our institutional leaders to buy into what we are doing. The need for internal marketing of the development process never ends.

Sometime in the 1980s I became familiar with Robert K. Greenleaf's concept of servant-leadership (1977). It seems to me that his idea has special application to people who work in philanthropy. We serve what we love. If we love mankind, we serve mankind. Ironically, I have discovered that in the process of serving through philanthropy, my work inevitably thrusts me into a leadership role. An attitude of service is the most effective path to leadership.

A long time ago I decided that my talents and skills could be used best in the organization to plant a few new ideas here and there, and to initiate a new order in a quiet, prosaic, serving sort of way. At my comparatively low level of administration and influence, I've had a wonderful time trying to make things happen.

And, Murray might add, succeeding.

5

Advancing
the Profession:
The Philanthropic
Fundraiser
as Mentor

What shall I do with my life? How much am I
willing to give of myself, of my time, of my love?
—*Eleanor Roosevelt,*
as quoted in Lawson,
1991, p. 49

The "Giving Is Caring" calendar discussed in the previous
chapter came about through a mentoring relationship between Sheree Parris Nudd, a young woman not long out of
college, and Murray, the old-school, but up-to-date, professional more than thirty years her senior. Just after Murray
finished the Huguley Memorial Hospital campaign, the hospital's development department experienced a leadership crisis, with several directors coming and going in a short period
of time. Nudd had just finished a two-year, entry-level communications internship in the development and public relations office when the hospital administration shocked her by
asking her to take the directorship of the entire department.
She recalls:

During my internship, I had usually worked on the public relations side, so the only thing I knew about Milton Murray was an image I had of a white-haired man with a briefcase and a loud voice who would swoop into the office from time to time to talk with the fundraising staff.

He must have been annoyed that despite his best efforts to secure a mature, seasoned development professional in the hospital, the administration had turned the operation over to a twenty-four-year-old, just two years out of college. But he never showed any disappointment, although he admits now that the possibility had crossed his mind that I wouldn't work.

After leading the original $3.25 million campaign for the hospital, Milton continued his relationship with Huguley as a consultant. He had spent three years building up good relations in the community, and I knew enough to listen to him. What he said, we did. It started working. We wrote some proposals, we visited some foundations, and, with Milton's constant encouragement, I began to see that I could really like this work.

I was in a very steep learning curve, and Milton was a willing teacher. I'd present him with an idea and he'd offer suggestions or a new angle, based on his long experience. He always did it in a manner that made it seem as though we were collaborators. Even when he could have saved time by telling me the answer, he made the effort to lead me through the learning process. I learned much faster than if I had been on my own, just reading fundraising texts and attending conferences.

My advice to college students and young professionals is to find yourself a mentor, someone with whom you can develop a professional learning relationship. Don't wait for someone to discover you. Search out that person yourself, and then take the responsibility for developing and pursuing that mentoring relationship.

Nudd attributes her own professional success in the years since then to many things, including supportive, development-oriented administrators. But at the top of the list she credits the time and interest Murray took to help her learn the ropes.

According to Murray, leadership can come from any quarter and he is particularly eager to see it come from the younger generation. The first solid generation of professionals in American philanthropy is now essentially retired. Many of them, like Murray, moved into the field at midcareer from public relations, journalism, business, or administrative jobs. Murray wants to see young people commit themselves to a career in philanthropy right out of college. But he faces a problem. Philanthropy is a new enough specialty that few schools offer classes in the subject, let alone majors or even concentrations of courses in a broader curriculum. Consequently, students rarely are confronted with the option of studying for a career in this field. They flock to other comparatively obscure career specializations in technology and the sciences primarily because these vocations have achieved the identity and assumed status of a bona fide "major." Yet right across the campus in the administration building, employees are happily earning very respectable salaries in a work that demands professional-level skills in communication, management, and even psychology. In many cases their work puts them at the heart, or at least the stomach, of the institution's mission. Murray's dream and his challenge is to expose young people to philanthropy in their college years.

In 1985 he turned his wishes into leadership action. Development offices in the institutions with which he consults run on notoriously tight budgets. Murray knew that few of these offices could hire interns simply for the noble goal of promoting the profession. Yet those were the places where young people could really catch the vision and inspiration of philanthropy. Working with several major donors and church leaders, he established a $600,000, five-year fund to support summer student internships in development offices at Adventist colleges and hospitals. The fund also reimbursed participating institutions for half the cost of full-time, first-year development employees just out of college. Since the program was established, nearly fifty college students have completed summer internships in development and thirty entry-level positions have been funded. As of 1990, sixteen professionals were working in philanthropy around the United States who got their start through Murray's STEP-UP program.

Murray's office publishes a quarterly newsletter for the interns. Michael Jaquez, a 1990 summer intern at one institution, attended Murray's 1990 triennial philanthropy conference in Indianapolis as part of his internship. He wrote in to the newsletter:

> The Conference changed my outlook on philanthropy. I must confess my outlook was less than favorable. I am pursuing a double major in public relations and institutional development, but I had not seriously considered a career in fundraising.
>
> I viewed fundraisers as a form of parasite. I thought rich people must cringe when the development officer walked into the room. Gradually, my negative view began to change as I worked in the development office at my college and during my summer STEP-UP internship. It was meeting 160 dedicated fundraisers face to face at the conference that finally changed my mind. These people are not parasites. They care about other people. They believe in the missions of their institutions. They look at fundraising as benefiting not only the receiver of the gift, but the giver as well.
>
> The conference taught me that philanthropy is not about money. It's about people.

Indeed, philanthropy is about helping people. But Murray, in practicing his vocation, sometimes chooses to "help" people, particularly young employees, in ways that—his critics might claim—add a curious new meaning to the word. To appreciate the best example, which has become part of Murray folklore, the reader must understand the polite politics of personnel administration and job recruitment in the large system of Adventist institutions, including hospitals, colleges, and universities; primary and secondary schools; the ministry; and administrative units. As diversified and apparently autonomous as these institutions are, they operate on an unwritten code of cooperation when it comes to handling employees. Thus, for example, when a church-run hospital in California wants to hire a business teacher from a church-run college in Tennessee to be vice president for financial operations, the hospital will usually call the college president or dean and ask for "permission to talk" to the teacher. If the college president demurs, the hospital will, according to the code, graciously look elsewhere for a new vice president, and that will be the end of the matter.

Two days before his graduation from Pacific Union College with a communications degree in the spring of 1982, twenty-two-year-old David Colwell had a job interview with Milton Murray. Colwell initially had little interest in the job Murray had to offer. The first problem was that it was on the East Coast, and he wanted to stay in California. Second, although the job had a heavy emphasis on editorial duties, it had something to do with fundraising, which he didn't know much about. Colwell had his heart set on a career in health care public relations.

> Milton offered me the job on the spot, but I knew I had another interview in a few days for a staff position on an in-house newspaper at Loma Linda University. I said, "Let me think about it for a week." He agreed. I went to the other interview and got a job offer at a salary substantially higher than the one Murray offered. At the same time, I knew that this second job wasn't exactly what I was looking for either.
>
> Meanwhile, Murray had helped me to see the broader possibilities for growth in the job he was offering. After some typical salary negotiation, I took the job.

Even today, when Milton and I joke about my original interview, he claims he made it clear that he wanted a minimum two-year commitment. I never heard that or, if he said it, it never made an impression. And I remind him that his letter of employment didn't say anything about it.

About a year and a half into his work for Murray in Washington, D.C., Colwell was contacted by the health care management corporation serving Adventist hospitals in California. They wanted Colwell to run corporate communications and invited him to visit for an interview. According to Colwell, the West Coast corporation had followed good form, had contacted Murray for "permission to talk," and had received it.

Colwell recalls: "One morning I told Milton I was setting up an appointment to go out to California. He said, 'What do you think you're doing? You can't leave here. You've got a two-year commitment and you've only been here fifteen months.' Well, I had no idea that I had ever made such a commitment. If I had, I would have kept it. I'm a man of my word."

Colwell had his heart set on returning to California. The job was his and the interview a mere formality. Inexplicably, Murray had given "permission to talk," and yet he was objecting when Colwell appeared to want the job.

Murray had miscalculated. He had assumed that young Colwell, who might be flattered by the initial attention, would ultimately turn the job down when he was forced to make a decision. Murray was wrong, and he had to work fast to recover. Today he tells the story with a "you'll probably think this is terrible but here are the facts" blush and a shrug. "I couldn't lose David," he insists. "And he should have known that it wouldn't have been good for his career to make a move like that. I did the only thing I could do. I called the president of the church's North American division and explained the problem. He called the president of the West Coast health care management corporation, who told his man to retract the job offer to Colwell. That took care of it."

All this happened in a single workday, and by the end of the day, Colwell was dazed and hurt. And flattered. He says, "I had my heart set on going back to California. I felt kind of bad. I really wasn't angry at Milton, because I got to thinking that maybe this was the best thing. Milton's lectures made me think about commitment. And I felt good that he went to all that trouble to make sure that I stayed."

For his part, Murray, who sometimes walks where angels fear to tread, is not bashful about expounding on his obligation to give seasoned advice, or, in this case, even to arrange events, if a young professional is about to make a mistake.

When you accept a job in the professional world, you have to know that your boss, if she or he is worth anything at all, is going to take an active interest in your career development, not as your master, but as your mentor. That means there is going to be a kind of parental concern.

I thought that David should stay in his job for a minimum of two years. I think that any young person should stay in his or her first job out of college for at least that length of time. Recently, some of my colleagues said, "Murray, you're too easy on them. You should be saying five or six years." To which I said, "I've been saying five or six years for many years, but I was shouted down so often that I relented and came down to two or three. I've been in favor of five or six all along."

Even if you start a job and discover that it isn't what you wanted, I think that you should stick with it. It doesn't do your reputation or your habits any good to be jumping around. There is always something to learn, wherever you are. Even if, on your first day on the job, they say to you, "Welcome to the development office. Your first job is to take this rag and bucket and clean those baseboards"—*do it*. And do it cheerfully and well. Before long, they'll have you stuffing envelopes! If you have a good disposition, and you remain interested despite the initial dullness, there is no limit to where you can go. But you have to be adaptable and be willing to do whatever needs to be done. It's that simple. And if your boss takes events into her or his own hands to see that you learn that lesson, at least be grateful for that interest in your career.

Colwell remained with Murray for seven more years. Much to Murray's delight, Colwell's career goals changed. In 1991, he moved back to California at last, to work at Loma Linda University Medical Center, not as director of communications, but as director of development. Colwell says he is glad that Murray torpedoed the original California opportunity. "I appreciate Milton's looking out for me and helping me to establish some continuity in my work. In the following seven years, I grew in my job and my career. I feel that I am better prepared for what I want to do in my life than I would have been if I had left at that time. Later, Milton often assured me that after I had worked with him the appropriate length of time he would do anything to help me find the job I wanted. And he's done that."

Murray admires the potential of youth, relentlessly seeks to attract fledgling college graduates into the profession, and has built a professional staff in his office whose average age is in the late twenties. At the same time, Murray is out of step in an age of business that, for a time at least, has glorified rapid upward mobility among young professionals. In Murray's hall of fame, there are few whiz-kids.

If a young woman comes to an organization claiming that she wants to make a contribution to the program, she should stay there long enough to make that contribution. Many times we see something different. Perhaps she came in as an assistant director. In six months' time she's wondering why she isn't an associate director. Then there's a shuffle and she lets people know that she'll be hurt if she isn't made director. Pretty soon she's gone to take a vice presidency at another organization. And we all say, "Wow, she's really somebody." Maybe she is, but it's too early to tell. Will she be a significant professional in the long haul?

A few years ago I heard Richard Taft, then owner of Taft Publications, tell a story at a convention. A young man graduated from college and the development office at his alma mater took him on in some kind of entry-level position. Within a very short time they made him assistant to the corporation and foundation officer. Pretty soon he became that officer. Before long he was assistant vice president and then vice president of the college. All this happened in a very short time—maybe three or four years. His salary rose from $22,000 to $37,000. A real whiz-kid. He made a tremendous impression on people. The medical center across town heard about him and offered him a vice presidency at $55,000. Of course, he took it. His wife was proud of him. His mother was proud of him. His college probably wrote profiles about him, accompanied by photos of him in a trendy power suit, for its slick recruitment publications. He was somebody.

Six months after our young hero accepted the new vice presidency across town, the medical center fired him for incompetence. He didn't have the experience or the seasoning. He had "made it" on a smile and a shoeshine, on the coattails of other people in the office who really knew what they were doing, and on the well-meaning but misguided assistance of faculty and administrators who liked him and wanted him to succeed.

People in positions like mine have a responsibility not to allow that tragedy to happen to young professionals or to the work of philanthropy. The well-being of too many other people who can be benefited by this work is at stake.

Murray's experiences with Nudd and Colwell, recounted earlier, are illustrations of his career-long practice of helping—or even coercing—others, especially the young, to catch the vision. He is not a professional snob. Instead, he cultivates the philanthropic spirit wherever he finds it. Thus he agitates for, and admires, the participation of youth and amateurs as much as that of young professionals.

He expresses his admiration by pointing to stories where youthful enthusiasm more than made up for a lack of any theoretical knowledge of fundraising. His own father, Walter Murray, provided his son with a fine example of this. To understand the story, one must understand the context, for it could have been repeated, and probably was, in a hundred similar circumstances and institutions across America.

In 1919, Berrien Springs, Michigan, was a small college town—that is, a small town with a small college. It had once been the most important town in the county, but twenty-five years before it had ceased to be the county seat, and it regained only a portion of its prestige eight years later when Seventh-day Adventists built Emmanuel Missionary College, the only college in the county, on a farm about a mile north of the main village.

The simple campus offered a few wooden frame buildings scattered informally along a strikingly formal double row of young Norwegian spruces, which had been planted fifteen years earlier in the middle of former cornfields by the school's foresighted founder. The student body of three hundred came predominantly from the farms or smaller cities of the Great Lakes region and upper Midwest. Campus life, including recreation, social activity, academic pursuits, and a good deal of manual labor, was governed by a conservative outlook that, even by the practices of the time, seemed quaint, if not prudish. In the process, however, it bound the students and their teachers into a happy, tight-knit society.

Students came to EMC because they valued the school's keen sectarian, service-oriented spirit, still glowing fervently in the embers of the great Protestant college missionary movement of the 1890s through the 1920s. Walter Murray was a fine specimen of the earnest, sturdy, level-headed graduate this missions-oriented college was founded to produce. He also exemplified the determination many students needed in attempting to receive a college education at Berrien Springs and at many other small church-related colleges in early twentieth-century America.

He had been raised by his mother in Davenport, Iowa, after his father was killed by the kick of a horse when Walter was twelve. He earned his way through Adventist boarding academies in Iowa, Illinois, and Michigan by working on the school farms or in their boiler plants. In 1915, he enrolled at EMC, paying his way by working eight to ten hours a day in the college business office as an accountant and cashier, and fitting whatever classes he could around his work schedule. Not surprisingly, his grades were unremarkable and he was not much of a campus socialite. But his industriousness allowed him to complete his coursework in four years, be elected president of his senior class in the 1918–19 school year, and become well acquainted with Golda James, who was finishing the liberal arts course.

In February of that year, he and Golda, by then his fiancée, were asked by Adventist World Headquarters to go to South America as missionaries upon their graduation. They well understood the implications of "the call." It meant leaving behind everything they knew and loved and devoting years of service, maybe even their entire lives, to the "cause" in a foreign land. But they also knew that this was precisely the work for which they had each prepared. They accepted.

In the same month, college president Frederick Griggs called Walter into his office to approach him about another more immediate assignment. The president wanted a new music building and he had few traditional options for securing the necessary $6,000. Throughout his long career in the years ahead as a mission administrator, Walter Murray would never consider himself a fundraiser. Yet as a senior college student, he was to lead one of the most remarkable fundraising campaigns in the history of that school, now called Andrews University, where his son Milton, sixty-six years later, would receive an honorary doctorate for significant fundraising achievements of his own.

As recorded in the college history (Vande Vere, 1972, p. 147), the president many years later recalled:

> I told Walter that the students could raise that [$6,000] in three months by soliciting friends and those whose names they could secure far and near. As I talked, I grew enthusiastic and told him I was sure they could raise the money in two months. I got more enthusiastic and told him I knew they could raise it in thirty days. Then I told him that he should lead in the matter. . . . I suggested that the evening worship two days later could be taken by the faculty for a concert, and that he should give a speech on the necessity of the music building and propose that the students build it.
>
> Well, all this made poor Walter groan. He very strongly questioned the ability of the students to raise $6,000 in thirty days, and more seriously questioned his ability to lead in such a movement.

Nevertheless, duty called and Walter Murray answered. The teachers gave their concert, Murray gave his speech, and the students, catching his enthusiasm, immediately organized a ways and means committee to plot strategy. Two weeks later Murray presided at the formal campaign kickoff, held at the college assembly. President Griggs reminded the students that the Children of Israel gave of their means to build the wilderness tabernacle so liberally that Moses eventually had to tell them to stop giving. Not to be outdone in the use of inspiring biblical illustrations, Murray compared the three-hundred-member student body with Gideon's army of three hundred men, who wrought a great victory over the huge and hated Midianite forces. The student newspaper paraphrased Murray as saying: "Though our task of raising $6,000 in thirty days might also look as out of proportion to our size, we could have the same success if we went about it in the same spirit" ("New Music Building Forms $6000 Goal," 1919, p. 1).

On March 30, with the campaign goal clearly in sight, Griggs and Murray staged a groundbreaking ceremony for the new building. Murray made yet another speech in which he emphasized that "many of us owe what we are to our college. It has led us to nobler, purer, and higher lives. EMC has made us know ourselves, and the only way we can thank her and her faithful teachers is to make this work our work" ("Breaking the Ground," 1919, p. 2).

Griggs told the students, with a tacit reference to the vocational purposes of the school, that "a missionary's education is not complete without music, and the more the better" ("Breaking the Ground," 1919, p. 22). Ironically, later in life Walter Murray acknowledged that his arduous work-study program during his college years and not the lack of proper facilities had prevented him from studying music.

Students solicited their relatives and friends all over the country; held auctions; sold popcorn, peanuts, and brooms; and engaged in a host of other schemes to meet their individual and collective goals. Twenty-eight days after the campaign was launched, and two days early, the students achieved their goal amid thunderous celebration in the college chapel.

More than seven decades later, Walter Murray's son notes that $6,000 in thirty days would be a remarkable achievement for three hundred undergraduates at any time. But for perspective, one must remember that, according to the Consumer Price Index, $6,000 in 1919 could buy what would require $47,000 in 1991. If the two thousand undergraduates at the same school attempted a proportional achievement today, they would face a thirty-day goal of $315,000.

Another of Murray's favorite examples of amateur philanthropic accomplishment occurred on another college campus in the early 1970s. At that time the Ford Foundation sponsored Murray to provide consulting services for several institutions in Latin America, including the Centro de Enseñanza Técnica y Superior (CETYS), a business college in Mexicali, Mexico. Murray knew the fundraising environment well, having served full time at Guadalajara from 1964 to 1967 under another Ford Foundation sponsorship.

Students at CETYS decided that the school needed an auditorium. They asked Alfonso Marín-Jiménez, one of Murray's clients and the director of public relations and development, what could be done to get one. According to Murray, Marín-Jiménez was not optimistic.

Marín-Jiménez told the students that a new building would cost $125,000 and that the university was hard pressed just to operate at its present level. The administration could do nothing to make their dream come true. So the students said, "We'll raise the money ourselves. We've raised money for a bus and we've raised money for a flagpole. Why can't we raise money for an auditorium?"

The administration agreed to endorse the effort if the half-dozen student leaders, aged eighteen to twenty-two years, agreed to stay with the project to its completion. With this support, the students went back to Marín-Jiménez and asked, "What do we do first?" He told them that they had to prove their belief in the project by making financial commitments themselves, beyond the time they were investing to lead the campaign. He said, "Come back in a week and tell me what you are going to do out of your own pockets."

When they went back to Marín-Jiménez a week later, he had them put their pledges, totaling about $200, in writing. He put the documentation in a file in his desk. "Don't forget," he said. "This is your commitment."

Then he told them that they had to organize the student body by recruiting about sixty students as potential campaign volunteers, inspiring them with the idea and securing more pledges. Two weeks later the leaders returned to Marín-Jiménez with more pledges, and he helped them to set goals for the whole student body, the faculty, and the administration.

Once it was organized, the campaign throughout the school went quickly. The sixty recruits became leaders, raised $3,000 from the students, and used some bold techniques on the faculty. They solicited teachers in front of classrooms filled with students. Any teacher who seemed reluctant was reminded by the solicitor that the poor students were contributing. Faculty donations reached $5,000.

At the same time, leaders convinced a fruit juice distributor to sell them juice at half cost. For two days CETYS students swarmed the streets of Mexicali, selling the juice for double the regular retail cost, making a 400 percent profit, and netting $3,000. A similar venture with ball-point pens brought in $2,400.

The next step was to get alumni to contribute, but that wasn't easy. CETYS had only been in operation about twelve years, so the majority of graduates were just beginning their careers. Young alumni in any institution are traditionally the weakest supporters; in addition, the concept of alumni support for educational institutions was extremely new in Mexican higher education. In spite of this double problem, the student leaders raised $15,000, which was good considering the circumstances.

Next they took on the business community, which they were counting on for the bulk of their support. They started by going to the owner of one of the nicer restaurants in the city, explaining that they were students at CETYS who were leading in the campaign to build an auditorium for the school. After describing how the students and faculty had supported the campaign, they said, "The development of the university has spin-off effects for you and we'd like you to do something. We'd like you to make a small room or a large table available in your restaurant one night a week for about twenty weeks. We are going to bring in eight or ten businesspeople each week from the Mexicali area and solicit them for support. Your contribution will be the series of dinners."

The owner agreed and they began the process,

working on the owners of furniture stores, gas stations, tailor shops, and other small businesses. After the dinner they showed slides and made their appeal. All but one of the businesspeople made contributions; with an average gift of $400, the total raised came to $46,000.

This effort brought the total campaign up to $75,000 and exhausted most of the potential in the Mexicali area. The students wondered where they should turn next. This is when I started advising them. They asked if there would be any money available from corporations or foundations in the United States. I said, "There aren't many in the United States that are interested in Latin America. But we might try the Kresge Foundation. It gives to brick-and-mortar projects."

So that became my job. I wrote the proposal for the students and showed them what I was doing and why. When the proposal was finished, the students just sent it off with a cover letter. Nobody went to Troy, Michigan, to talk to anybody in the foundation.

At that time there was a woman working at the Kresge Foundation named Betty MacGuire, whom I had come to know from other contacts. As she read the proposal, which, as far as she knew, was written by these students at Mexicali, she noticed that CETYS was listed as a member of ACPRA. She called John Leslie, executive director of ACPRA, and asked him about CETYS. He said, "I don't know much about it, but you should call Murray."

So she called me, and I realized that I needed to be up-front with her about my involvement in the proposal. I said, "Betty, I'll be happy to tell you about CETYS, but you should know that I'm consulting with that school and I wrote the proposal you are considering." She said, "I appreciate your mentioning that, Milton, and I understand your position. But tell me about the school." So I did.

A few weeks later, the students got a letter from Kresge telling them that CETYS would receive $25,000, contingent on their raising the last $25,000. The students already knew that they had more work to do, so while they waited to hear from Kresge, they zeroed in on an airline official at the Mexicali airport. They told him that they were raising money for their university and how they were doing it, and they ended by asking the airline to help by giving them five round-trip flight tickets to Mexico City. When the airline official replied that he was not authorized to do that, they answered, "Whatever time it takes, we'll wait." He told them to come back in a week.

A week later they went back, and the official promised them their tickets. A short time later the students went to Mexico City to see the chairman of the board of the Banco Nacional de México—the largest bank at that time in Latin America.

They didn't have an appointment; they simply walked into the secretary's office and said that they wanted to see the chairman of the board. When the secretary pointed out that the chairman was a very busy man, the students countered by saying, "We came all the way from Mexicali to see him. We *must* see him."

When it became obvious to the students that they weren't making much progress with the secretary (who, in all fairness, was trying to be helpful), they said, "We want to give you this little present for trying to help us." One of the students produced a bottle of perfume from a bag and placed it gently on her desk. She said, "Wait in the hall and I'll see what I can do." Within an hour the students were in the chairman's office. They left with a commitment for $50,000.

Incredibly, they had pulled it off. With guidance from their elders, some home-grown ideas of their own, and a lot of nerve, they raised $150,000 for their school. That's the kind of story that almost makes me cry. That's real-life philanthropy at its best.

Some might argue with me on this point. They might say that these students, or those in my father's thirty-day campaign in 1919, were working in their own self-interest. Look a little closer and you will see that this is not true. Remember that my father never had a chance to take music when he was a student. The campaign occurred two months before he graduated. He never had the opportunity to use the building as a student. Similarly, the CETYS students recognized that they would be long gone before their auditorium was finished. Their enthusiasm cannot be called self-interest; they worked for benefits that would fall only to others, and they knew it.

Throughout the published histories of many colleges, particularly private ones, you can find the record of similar, exciting, student-led campaigns. Unfortunately, you usually *only* find them in the history books. We hear of fewer and fewer examples in higher education today. Why?

The most simplistic answer, and therefore the most questionable, is that students of today are too self-centered, too materialistic, too lazy, too, too, too. If this is true, how did they get that way? Is it possible that, institutionally, we did not provide good role models? I think so. We have, for the most part, turned philanthropic fundraising in our colleges entirely over to professionals like me and have cut out the students entirely. When is the last time you heard of a college president like Frederick Griggs hauling in the senior class president and saying, "I want you to lead a student campaign to raise $315,000. And I want it done in thirty days."

It is possible that the college students of today don't wage the great campaigns of the past for the same reason that many potential donors don't give: nobody asks.

Yes, it is a lot neater to have the professionals handle everything, and many nonprofit organizations should keep it that way. But a college, of all places, is where young people should learn and grow in goodness and truth. What better way to accomplish that purpose than to involve them in the philanthropic process?

Of course, times *do* change, and methods must be adjusted to the times. That is why I am delighted to see many colleges involving students, either as volunteers or paid workers, in phonathon campaigns for their annual fund. But perhaps that should only be the beginning.

No matter what may be said about this or any other generation, I believe that almost every young heart retains some reservoir of altruism, however small, that can be tapped for the good of the institution and society. As leaders and educators, it is our opportunity and obligation to do the tapping. Mentoring should be an important part of the agenda for every professional in philanthropy.

6

Finding the Creative Solution: The Philanthropic Fundraiser as Innovator

I have learned that it is just as important, and rewarding, to help a great leader to function as it is to be one.

—*Greenleaf, 1979, p. 110*

Five hundred dollars! *Five hundred dollars!!?* This was an insult and an outrage! Corporate support was critical to the success of the campaign, and Alcon Laboratories—one of the largest ophthalmological pharmaceutical companies in the nation—was pivotal to encouraging other companies in Fort Worth, Texas, to support the proposed hospital. Physically, the company was one of the closest to the hospital construction site—just three miles down the road. One of the company founders was even a member of the eight-person campaign committee.

Murray had asked for $50,000 and he got $500.

The campaign for Huguley Memorial Hospital proved to be an interesting challenge for Murray. It started when a wealthy Dallas dentist, Herbert Taylor Huguley, left his estate, valued at about $3 million, to the Seventh-day Adventist Church in the late 1960s to build a hospital, presumably in Dallas, in honor of his parents. Murray recalls:

> Church administrators explored some possibilities in the Dallas area for a while. By the time the estate cleared the courts, an enterprising group of developers and Chamber of Commerce people in Fort Worth had heard about the Huguley gift and the Adventists' plan for it. The timing was interesting, because the developers in the rival city had recently received a recommendation from a prestigious consulting firm, urging them to build a hospital on the south side of Fort Worth. A hospital would be a big help in attracting business to the large undeveloped acreage in that area.
>
> The Chamber of Commerce man promoting business development was Bill Shelton. He took Chamber president Tom Law with him on a visit to the church's regional leadership and promised to help raise money if the proposed hospital ended up in Fort Worth instead of Dallas.
>
> Later, Shelton told me that he was interested in working with Adventists because his mother had been in and out of Hinsdale Hospital, near Chicago, for years. She loved the hospital, she loved the people there, and when Shelton had visited her, he was highly impressed with the way it was run.
>
> The campaign steering committee for the new hospital, which at the time existed only on paper, was made up of important community and business leaders. One of them was William Conner, chairman and one of the founders of Alcon.
>
> I had been told that Fort Worth was a tough town in which to raise money from corporations. At the time, there was a perception that corporations would have to contribute very little, because the two major foundations, Amon G. Carter and Sid Richard-

son, would look after most of the worthy projects. The hospital needed both the foundations *and* the corporations. We were trying to raise $3.25 million from the community, the largest hospital campaign the community had ever attempted. I couldn't expect all of it to come from the foundations. In fact, some members of the committee thought that we wouldn't get much from the foundations either.

When I had conducted the initial feasibility study, I had gone to see Conner. He was very cordial and was interested in the proposed hospital. He had traveled around the world, was acquainted with the church's hospitals in different places, and thought highly of them. And he had agreed to help. When the time came to approach his company I had great aspirations. After all, Conner was on the campaign committee, and his company was practically adjacent to the hospital. I thought in terms of $100,000. After more research, I reduced my expectations to $50,000 and felt confident that it was a solid, reasonable request.

We soon got a letter back saying that the Alcon contributions committee had studied our proposal and had decided to give us $500. I was stunned.

I went back to see Conner, showed him the letter, and said, "This is a real surprise. You are a key person on the campaign committee. You're one of the pillars. If you represent one of the leading operations in this town, and this is indicative of the kind of support we're going to get from the others, we might as well close up right now."

Conner laughed. Finally he said, "I know I shouldn't be laughing. This is a serious matter. I'll tell you what happened. I don't personally make this kind of decision. We have a committee that handles these requests. Apparently it didn't receive enough background information or didn't understand the seriousness of what we are trying to do. But Milton, you should also know that we don't give to brick and mortar. That's our company policy."

Well, I *hadn't* known that, and I should have done better at digging up that information. After all, it's the heart of my business to be aware of things like that. For some inexplicable reason, this detail had eluded me, but Conner had known all along. This posed a serious problem, because our whole campaign was for brick and mortar. But Bill is a great man and he said, "Milt, let me think about this for a while. You may be able to come up with a solution."

I left Conner's office and began to do some fast thinking. Alcon's participation in the campaign was critical to the momentum of continued corporate participation. The company didn't give to brick and mortar and yet the campaign to build the hospital had not been designed for any other kind of gift money. It was doubtful that Conner would want to ask his committee for a variance in company policy. The only other option would be to create a program that would be directly meaningful to the mission and future growth of the hospital and that would also be attractive to Conner and his committee. What could that be?

Murray had a thorough understanding of the history and philosophy of Adventist health care. From their inception in the 1860s, when John Harvey Kellogg's Battle Creek Sanitarium was established, Adventist hospitals had focused heavily on health education and preventive medicine, particularly as they related to diet, life-style, and dependency issues. Murray had also discovered by chance that a key to Conner's appreciation for these hospitals around the globe was his respect for their philosophical emphasis on health. In the more reflective moments of his disappointment over Alcon's $500 rebuff, Murray recalled conversations in which Conner had expressed his admiration for the Adventist life-style and the church's position on alcohol and tobacco. This was at a time when both drugs had little of the rapidly developing popular stigma they hold in American society today.

Eureka! Creativity often blossoms under pressure, and Murray rediscovered the maternal relationship between necessity and invention.

> I went back to Conner a week later and said, "Bill, I have an idea. You are the first person I am telling. What would you think about Alcon doing something to help this new hospital launch a health education program as soon as it opens? You know as well as I do that we are great advocates of health education. But you also know that once we get involved in building the hospital, dealing with clinicians and doctors, and worrying about bed counts and occupancy rates, it may be three years or even ten years before we get moving in health education. I know that you are interested in this area and that you might be able to help accelerate the process. And it wouldn't be for brick and mortar. It's program oriented, so it fits your guidelines. I'd have to get special permission from the administration to allow you to do something in this area, because we're supposed to be raising money for brick and mortar. But what's $25,000 in comparison to $3 million? Furthermore, it's extremely important for others to know that your company has participated."
>
> Conner said, "That's a good idea. Write it up."
>
> I went to the administrator, Bill Wiist, and said, "We're at an impasse with Alcon. We're going to get $500, and maybe if we ask them each year, we can pick up another $500. But it is essential that we do a lot better. I'd like to see the hospital administration and the board commit itself to developing a health education program within weeks after the hospital opens. I think we can get $25,000, $5,000 a year, from Alcon for such a program if you chip in something for the first years. That way, we can involve Alcon right from the start."

Wiist agreed, and Murray hammered out a proposal to Alcon and a program plan for the hospital. Within weeks, the idea was approved by everyone. When the hospital opened in 1977, the administration kept its word, backed by the grant from Alcon. Classes in health and fitness, nutrition, and birthing techniques, an innovation in hospital services in Fort Worth at the time, put Huguley Hospital on the map of community approval and gave it an immediate public profile disproportionate to its size among its larger, better-established competitors around the city. According to Sheree Parris Nudd, then an entry-level public relations staffer at the hospital, positive response and participation far exceeded expectations. Because of a lack of designated space, the seminars, lectures, and demonstrations were held on week nights in the small hospital cafeteria until the staff tired of setting the chairs up each time. Lamaze birthing classes were held in the corridors. A single lecture about fiber in the diet by a professor from the Loma Linda University School of Public Health drew nearly three hundred people.

The initial and almost immediate popularity of the health education program helped to shape the next fundraising campaign, launched within five years after Huguley's opening. An $11.5 million expansion program included $3.4 million for a separate health education complex, which has helped to define the hospital's identity and mission in the Fort Worth community. Murray wonders how things might have been different: "When Bill Conner and I get together, we still laugh about that $500 letter. It really did something for Huguley. Suppose that Alcon, under pressure from Bill, had violated its company policy by giving us $25,000 for brick and mortar. The company's name would be etched on a plaque along with a hundred other company names somewhere on the donor wall, but where would health education be? Sometimes negatives can become positives!" Murray's creative spirit, ingenuity, and calculated strategy had turned a dead-end proposition into a singular success.

In *The Charitable Impulse,* James Joseph (1989, p. 29) affirms the distinction between creativity and innovation, as defined by Theodore Levitt, a Harvard marketing professor. Levitt maintains that creativity means "thinking up new things" and innovation means "doing new things." Joseph uses both concepts in his discussion of Eugenio Mendoza, the great twentieth-century Venezuelan developer, industrialist, and philanthropist. (Interestingly, Milton Murray had significant occasion to admire, at close range, Mendoza's creative and innovative qualities when Murray advised and assisted him in forming the Universidad Metropolitana in Caracas, Venezuela, in the early 1970s.)

Accepting Levitt's model, the observer can recognize both characteristics in Murray. His creative solution to the apparent impasse with Alcon Laboratories put health education in a favored spot on Huguley Hospital's agenda, and someone else implemented the program. In the case of Murray's famous "Giving Is Caring" page-a-day philanthropy calendar, discussed in Chapter Four, he was both creator and innovator, conceiving the idea of putting philanthropy quotes in an existing and popular calendar format and following through with production and marketing. He is playing a similar dual role in his nationwide campaign for a postage stamp honoring philanthropy, discussed in Chapter Seven.

Although examples of Murray's raw creativity are numerous, it is as an innovator—the adapter and implementer of someone else's good idea—that he receives his greatest acclaim, at least from his immediate colleagues in his own organization. In the 1980s, Murray initiated challenge programs that directly or indirectly have been credited with generating more than $230 million for health care and secondary and higher education. These incentive programs rewarded participating institutions with sizable monetary grants if the institutions met specific fundraising goals.

In the 1970s, Adventists operated twelve colleges and universities in the United States and Canada, with enrollments ranging from six hundred to four thousand. In the corridors of church headquarters in Washington, D.C., and at conventions of church educational leaders around the country, Murray began to hear people say, "Our colleges need to raise $50 million dollars." When leaders began talking about raising money for these institutions, Murray knew that it wouldn't be long before they asked him to figure out how to do it. And he knew he would face a tough challenge.

The colleges, for the most part established in the late nineteenth century, had been slow to appreciate the value of endowments. Without that stabilizing influence, the 1970s found them facing heavy financial pressure from high inflation and burgeoning baby boom enrollments. Capital expansion was a high priority, yet students and their families could not be expected to pick up the cost through excessive tuition increases.

Nor could much be expected from alumni, or so it seemed. Alumni participation in annual fund giving lingered at a shabby 6 percent, far below the national average of about 25 percent. Murray recognized the special irony of this dismal alumni record, which could partially be explained by the fact that Adventists, as a group, are relatively generous givers. The *1978 Yearbook of American and Canadian Churches* (Abingdon Press, 1978, p. 266), for example, showed that with more than half a million U.S. members, Adventists maintained the highest per capita giving of forty-two reporting denominations, at least 400 percent higher than the Southern Baptist Convention, the Episcopal Church, the United Methodist Church, the Lutheran Church–Missouri Synod, the Lutheran Church in America, or the Christian Church (Disciples of Christ).

As a member himself, Murray understood this ethic of his fellow parishioners, who are encouraged to return 10 percent of their before-tax income to pay the salaries and costs of parish ministers and church administrators. Beyond this they are urged to contribute an additional 5 to 10 percent of their income to support worldwide programs, the local congregation, and its various ministries, including elementary and secondary schools. Perhaps because of this subcultural preoccupation with direct ecclesiastical contributions, members saw little need to support their alma maters, which they had attended at typically high, private-college cost and usually at great personal and family sacrifice. An equally valid and much simpler explanation for their low level of college annual fund support may be that they had never been asked.

Thus Murray could see a bad news/good news/bad news pattern: (1) members rarely gave to their colleges, (2) they had a strong tradition of giving, and (3) they may have reached the limits of their giving ability.

> I didn't know how to relate to that $50 million figure I kept hearing in church administrative circles. Someone had come up with it, and everybody seemed to be accepting it as gospel. Certainly nobody had talked to me about its feasibility. I didn't do anything about it for a while because I didn't know how to find $50 million dollars. Hospital campaigns for a few million dollars were one thing. This was altogether different, and I had learned throughout my career not to talk big until I knew what I was talking about. I had faced enough frustration in my career dealing with administrators who had been soured on philanthropy by big talkers, so I just did some quiet thinking about the problem to myself.

At about the same time, Murray was providing consulting services for Oakwood College, a historically black college of about 1,200 students in Huntsville, Alabama. The college had received an invitation from the Bush Foundation in Saint Paul, Minnesota, to send representatives to a one-day meeting in Atlanta to explain a new challenge program. The Oakwood development office asked Murray to join them.

The Bush Foundation originally had been interested primarily in higher education in the North Central United States. After years of awarding direct grants to colleges in that region, the foundation began exploring new and more effective ways of distributing its money. Most significantly, it had developed a program to assist historically black colleges in the South with alumni giving by awarding incentive or challenge grants for improvement in performance. When Oakwood officials went to Atlanta to learn about the Bush program, already in operation, Murray, as the college consultant, tagged along.

Humphrey Doermann, the president of the Bush Foundation, and two or three of his staff led out in this seminar for the dozen colleges that were represented. He told us that these colleges had been selected to be the recipients of awards the coming year, but that there were very specific guidelines.

Oakwood, like most of the church's colleges, had an extremely limited alumni giving program. That year the college had received $11,000 from 150 donors. The foundation promised that if alumni contributed a minimum of $24,000 beyond the $11,000 base the following year, it would match the increase dollar for dollar. Furthermore, the foundation would award $100 for each new donor up to a maximum of 240. In short, if the college simply raised an additional $24,000 and persuaded 390 people to make a minimum $5 gift, the foundation would reward Oakwood for its accomplishment with a $48,000 grant. It was a great deal, and a very meaningful inspiration for the college to get its alumni annual fund program in gear.

The Bush approach intrigued Murray because its track record at other schools seemed to provide an answer to a perplexing problem. He had joined the Adventist World Headquarters staff with the specific commission to raise money for health and educational institutions from sources outside the church and its membership. Finding the much-ballyhooed $50 million for the Adventists' North American higher education system was highly unlikely, because Murray knew that no significant outside monies from foundations or corporations would be forthcoming until the colleges had established a better record in raising money from their own constituencies. Why should the Kellogg or Kresge foundations take an interest in Loma Linda University or Andrews University, when the schools' alumni did not? Yet how could prevalent thinking be changed, significantly and *rapidly?* Church members weren't used to giving to their colleges, never had been, and had plenty of excuses not to begin now. Murray needed an exciting, high-profile means of grabbing their attention. Humphrey Doermann's idea might just be the answer. Once the church's colleges proved their competence in generating home-based support, they would be much more credible in their appeals to major foundations and corporations.

At the end of the day, I cornered Doermann and asked, "How much money do I need to do something of this kind for ten or twelve colleges?" He asked a few questions about the size of the schools and the number of alumni, and then he said, "You'd probably need a little over $2 million to do something similar to what we've been talking about here."

I left that meeting thinking about $2 million. Where could I get $2 million? Yet $2 million sounded a lot better to me—and more realistic—than $50 million. Granted, $2 million, even with its compounded effect through a program like Doermann's, wasn't going to solve all our problems, nor would it raise the entire $50 million. But it was a place to start. It was something we could do now!

I began to do some planning and sketched out how the money might be obtained over a five-year period—the length of a meaningful challenge program. The obvious sources for funding an incentive program like this were the church itself and a few heavy-duty donors, and it was clear that the amounts needed at any one time from these entities wouldn't be very large. As far as I am concerned, this is a tried and true principle of fundraising. If you make $42,000 a year and I ask you for $5,000 right now for a project, you'll say that it's impossible. But imagine instead that I tell you about a five-year program that deeply interests you, and that requires important, but not outrageous, commitments each year for five years. Remember, this is an idea that inspires you—scholarships for desperately needy students at your alma mater, for example.

You think about your wife and your children, the cabin on the lake you really want to buy, the car, however basic, that your son will need for college next year. But then you remember how you needed help when you went to college, and you pledge $1,000 a year for five years.

As the intermediary in this business of philanthropy I am successful because I've helped you accommodate the figure desired from you simply by not asking for it all at once. It becomes manageable and is within your mental limitations about giving. This is the same principle that the furniture salesperson uses, but for much more worthy ends. You are investing in humanity, not buying a headboard.

Murray went to the treasurer at the church headquarters and proposed the idea of raising a $2 million challenge fund for the colleges. The treasurer agreed that this was a good idea.

I said, "Of course, if we do this, the church will have to be involved. There isn't much virtue in going to private donors if you don't have the seal of approval from church leaders. And that seal of approval is money—an investment. Your involvement, right from the start, says that the project is important and alerts well-to-do business leaders to a genuine and meaningful opportunity. They will act if leadership shows the way."

The treasurer asked me how much I was talking about. I think he must have braced himself for a much higher figure, because when I suggested $75,000 a year for five years from all church entities, he seemed relieved and said that it shouldn't be a problem. Of course, none of this had been approved by any of the several committees that would eventually pass judgment on this proposal. But with the treasurer's support I had all the assurance I needed for the moment to begin broaching the subject to key donors.

With $375,000—nearly a fifth of the goal—already "in the pipeline," Murray approached the first donor, a couple in Southern California who owned a national first aid supply and equipment business and had expressed interest in supporting worthy endeavors.

In July 1979 I asked if I could stop by for a visit to talk about a venture that might interest them. We met at their home, and Mrs. Donor made us lunch. We chatted for a while about everything in general until, halfway through the meal, Mr. Donor—a no-nonsense, hard-driving, but very generous man—said, "Well, let's talk about something besides the weather. I know you're here to talk business. What do you want?"
I told them about Oakwood College and the Bush Foundation, and the possibility of doing something similar for our whole system of colleges. I also told them that the church was committed to the venture in a substantial way. I essentially asked for $600,000, but somehow Mr. Donor got the idea that I wanted $750,000. He used that figure several times in the conversation, and I didn't want to correct him. Mrs. Donor was a little hesitant, because they had just made a major commitment, their first ever, to a single college, and she didn't think they were ready to do more. She went into the kitchen and Mr. Donor, who must have sensed my concern, said, "We'll work out something. Don't worry."
When she returned, Mr. Donor said to her, "I think we can give him half of what he's asking. That would be $375,000." She agreed.
I was elated. Throughout my career I had raised millions from corporations, foundations, and private

donors after months of research and careful cultivation. This $375,000 was the most I had ever garnered
in an hour-and-a-half lunch.

With more than a third of the goal in hand, Murray
went to his superiors and asked for letters of introduction to
wealthy members who should be contacted. He made appointments with nearly three dozen over the next few months, pick-
ing up gifts ranging from $25,000 to $200,000.

By the following winter Murray remained $600,000
short, and the original Mr. Donor began to get impatient. He
didn't want his resources committed to a project that wasn't
going to happen. He began to talk about a deadline, the first
anniversary of his pledge.

Murray put his operation in high gear. In one week in
April 1980, he secured commitments from three donors for
$500,000. By July he was still short of the goal, but close
enough to satisfy Mr. Donor. By late summer the program
was announced to the college presidents, inaugurating the
Business Executives' Challenge to Alumni (BECA) program
during the 1980–81 school year.

Meanwhile, Murray had formed a group to devise the
structure of the challenge program and administer the distribution of awards. The nine-person committee included Robert Gale, president of the Association of Governing Boards of
Universities and Colleges; John Hall, vice president of CASE;
John Leslie, an educational consultant and former president
of CASE's predecessor, ACPRA; Gary Quehl, president of the
Council of Independent Colleges and later president of CASE;
three church officials; and two of the BECA major donors.

Murray selected 1979, when 6.5 percent of the 68,763
alumni of the North American Adventist colleges had contributed to the annual funds of their respective alma maters,
as the base year of the challenge program. The first year of
incentive awards generally called for a school to increase its
alumni participation by three percentage points, with a similar increase in total dollars contributed. That goal, if met,
would be matched dollar for dollar by a BECA grant. In addi-

tion, each new donor above the base-year total earned the college a grant ranging from $60 to $110.

Atlantic Union College, a liberal arts college of six hundred students in South Lancaster, Massachusetts, provided a typical example of the impact of Murray's program. In the base year 1979–80, AUC had raised $18,250 from 405 donors. In 1980–81, the first year of the challenge program, alumni unrestricted giving jumped to $38,089, an increase of nearly 110 percent. The number of donors increased by 60 percent to 649. The college earned a grant of $13,500 for the new dollars raised and $13,500 for the new donors. The increase was impressive for a small college and quickly attracted the attention of the administration and alumni. It was relatively easy money, but only for the first year. In the second year, Murray's administrative committee raised the goals higher while reducing the rewards for achieving them. Murray's purpose from the moment the program began was to wean the colleges from dependency on the challenge program by educating both the colleges and their alumni to get into the habit of alumni giving. By 1985, the end of the program's first phase, AUC had increased annual alumni giving from the base-year total of $18,250 to $89,435, nearly a 500 percent increase. Alumni participation in the annual fund jumped from 7.6 percent in 1980 to 30.2 percent in 1985. The other eleven colleges in the system saw similar progress.

From the beginning, Murray built the program on the concept of unrestricted giving. He believed that it was important to educate alumni to give for the simple principle of giving, instead of responding to specific appeals that caught their fancy in a capital campaign. According to Murray, the bread and butter of the annual fund must always come before the dessert of a capital campaign. Annual fund giving is essential to the day-to-day operation of the institution. If credited toward challenge goals, alumni gifts to capital campaigns would short-circuit the ongoing purpose of the annual fund.

It was a philosophy that the colleges subscribed to in theory but occasionally grumbled about in practice. Several of the schools were already in the midst of capital campaigns.

Nothing required them to participate in the challenge program and yet they were impressed by the potential monetary rewards. They complained, "How can we ask alumni to make unrestricted gifts to meet BECA goals and then expect them to turn around and give to our capital campaign?" Murray replied, in effect, "That's your problem," intimating that the awkwardness the colleges faced was simply the price they had to pay for running weak annual funds. Once alumni are educated to support the college systematically, he argued, their vision can be expanded to help meet specific capital needs as they arise. Any approach that works from the opposite direction is short-sighted, failing to build long-term loyalty and commitment.

Partway through the five-year program, Murray began enticing colleges to develop a network of volunteers—class agents—to assist with the annual fund. The idea had been around for decades in U.S. higher education, but the colleges Murray was working with had previously ignored the possibilities. John McKellip, a businessman from Minneapolis, prodded Murray into doing something about it. McKellip recalls:

> Milton had never had any contact with me before. He asked for an appointment, out of the blue, and I agreed to see him. He explained the challenge program and his enthusiasm and obvious vision inspired me, too. I suggested that nothing was going to happen unless we had alumni acting as volunteers themselves; then I told him of an experience I had nearly thirty-five years before that impressed me with the potential of getting alumni volunteers to do fundraising.
>
> During World War II, I attended the Navy flight training school in Corpus Christi, Texas. My roommate in the officers' quarters was a young man who had just graduated from Yale. For weeks at a time, he sat in our room at night writing letters, all by hand. When I asked him what it was all about, he said that he was a representative for his Yale graduating class and that he was attempting to stay in touch with a

portion of his classmates, maintain a sense of community among them, and encourage them to contribute
to the annual fund. He told me that the class repre-
sentative program was well established at Yale and
was highly effective in raising money for the school.

I told Milton that our church's colleges, because
of their size and specific mission, probably had even
more of a "family" atmosphere than Yale. The potential of a class agent program seemed even greater,
although nothing had ever been done about it. "But,"
I said, "in this day and age, you can't just give someone a bunch of envelopes and expect that to be
enough. The colleges will have to provide support with
a data base, record keeping, and word processing."

In classic fundraising form, Murray listened and let the
donor talk himself into a major gift. When everything was
settled, McKellip had contributed $200,000 for BECA, with a
portion of the gift designated for college development offices
that had no computer equipment to support a comprehensive
class agent program.

In 1980 Murray himself began serving as the agent for the
105 active members of the La Sierra College Class of 1949. In
ten years, under Murray's persistence and cajoling, his classmates contributed more than $68,000 to the annual fund. Dur-
ing the same period, alumni from the twelve colleges with
which Murray was consulting, including La Sierra, contributed
approximately $15 million to their respective alma maters. Mur-
ray was quick to point out to his classmates that if all college
classes in the system had contributed in proportion to theirs,
the collective total would have been more than $30 million.

The challenge grants for class agent programs yielded
quick results. Within two years, 70 percent of the classes in
the system were represented by a class agent who wrote at
least one letter a year to every classmate.

The initial five-year program ended in 1985. Collectively, alumni participation in college annual funds had jumped
from 6.5 percent to 27.3 percent, an increase of nearly 400

percent. Annual alumni contributions more than tripled, rising from $413,000 to $1.5 million.

Delighted with the results, church leaders and donors supported Murray's call for a three-year extension of the program. When the extension ended in 1988, the colleges' eight-year participation in BECA had wrought respectable alumni annual fund operations, supported by up-to-date record-keeping systems, well-organized phonathon campaigns, reasonable class agent performance, and a collective appreciation and enthusiasm for systematic philanthropic support.

Murray wasn't finished. In 1989 he announced a new four-year, $1 million incentive program for the colleges. Focusing on qualitative rather than quantitative aspects of philanthropic endeavor, the program broadened its influence from the relatively narrow domain of alumni participation in the annual fund to virtually all areas of development. It encouraged the colleges to write strategic plans, with measurable, time-related objectives for growth in specific areas. The plans and their execution, which required more subjective evaluation by a team of outside consultants, could earn top competitors rewards of up to $15,000. The evaluation process made broad allowances for the unique circumstances of each institution. Murray claimed to have no desire to force colleges into a predetermined mold based on some narrow philosophy for advancement offices. All he wanted was to see progressive planning and progressive results.

The revamped challenge program also rewarded the colleges for growth in the cultivation and solicitation of young alumni, improvement in overall volunteer programs, and a broader base and increased annual contributions among local business and industry.

Although the incentive dollars were highly attractive to most of the colleges in the system, there was still some grumbling, according to LuAnne Wolfe, Murray's associate and the day-to-day administrator of the program.

I received complaints from some of the schools about the nuisance of filing a strategic plan. This, of course, exactly illustrates the problem Milton is trying to correct. Schools that haven't established the habit of engaging in progressive planning must learn to do so. We are not asking any school to do anything it shouldn't already be doing, without the incentives. If the school doesn't want to write up a strategic plan, with measurable, time-related objectives, then it probably isn't doing its job.

Occasionally a seemingly fortunate school will have one or two big private or business donors who account for a large percentage of its total philanthropic support. The school may become lazy and rely on those few donors without developing a broad base of consistent, long-term support from other sources, including young alumni and other business and industry. Our incentive program does not reward development programs based on such narrow support, no matter how impressive the immediate dollar figures are.

Murray and Wolfe are fighting a tough battle. Development officers in higher education are hired to raise money *now*. The job turnover rates in the profession, particularly in smaller, less prestigious institutions, militate against stubborn long-range vision. A young career fundraiser, eager to advance in the profession, assumes, perhaps rightly, that future employers will be more likely to evaluate her performance by bottom-line dollar figures than by her contribution to the long-term success of the institution's financial advancement. Why shouldn't she be satisfied with making the immediate bottom line look good with a few big occasional gifts, even at the cost of an anemic future for an institution she will have long since left in the dust? The big occasional gifts are extremely important, Murray maintains, but no more so than the development of a solid base for future growth. Large gifts, as critical as they are, must never be allowed to cover a multitude of weaknesses in an annual fund program. Murray's program encourages an institution to recognize those weaknesses and correct them.

By 1986, with the BECA program established, some of Murray's colleagues and a donor or two suggested that he ought to start a similar program for the Adventists' large system of preparatory schools across the country, called "academies." Murray was hesitant. He had his hands full administering the BECA program with a minimal staff and he wasn't convinced that there was much possibility for success. The academies had an even weaker tradition of alumni giving than the colleges had had six years before. He was concerned that the schools didn't have enough basic personnel resources to start such a program. The returns would be too small in the first few years to justify hiring new staff. Simply stacking another job on the back of an already overworked teacher would never give the concept a fair chance of success.

Eventually he was persuaded, and he found himself pleased with the immediate support he received from donors and church leaders. In four years, the first seventeen schools in the program collectively increased their alumni gift income by 90 percent, their donor base by 122 percent, and their addressable alumni by 31 percent.

For years Murray has been a firm believer in the power of challenge programs to prime the philanthropic pump. The BECA program was a larger and more complex version of other challenge programs he had organized, including programs for the National Association for Hospital Development (now AHP) and NSFRE [see Chapter Four]. In 1979 he began a program similar to BECA for Adventist hospitals. At that time the church's health care system in the United States operated more than sixty hospitals representing 10,000 beds. Murray persuaded church leaders to establish the Hospital Development Fund to encourage annual and capital campaigns. In the first year, his meager $39,500 fund helped inspire four hospitals to complete campaigns totaling $3.5 million. By 1989 he had convinced church leaders to contribute $115,000 and the hospitals themselves to add $81,000 to the fund. This $196,000 successfully challenged twelve institutions to raise nearly $6 million that year. Typically, the challenge grants were awarded for a hospital's achievement of

some specific, time-related fundraising objective. By 1990 the
Hospital Development Fund had paid out nearly $1.4 million,
in grants ranging from $3,000 to $50,000, to challenge campaigns that collectively raised more than $32 million.

Murray is quick to acknowledge that some of this
money would have been raised without these programs, but
he firmly maintains that they helped, by exponential propor-
tions, to raise the profile, possibilities, and performance of
philanthropic activity for institutions and organizations that,
as a group, had been very slow to exploit their opportunities.
Murray believes, like James Joseph, in the creative, rather
than the preemptive, use of the philanthropic dollar. In *The
Charitable Impulse*, Joseph (1989, p. 170) argues that private
philanthropy, by itself, can never meet the total needs of
society. That's why we have governments. Philanthropy
works best when it acts as a catalyst in enterprises that are
outside the purview of public benevolence.

> Private philanthropy has served society so well because
> it has often been carefully targeted for maximum
> impact, invested the same way we invest our business
> dollars—to ensure maximum return. Some of the most
> thoughtful observers of philanthropic practices see
> effective philanthropy as analogous to the research
> and development budget of a business corporation.
> They point out that when the business enterprise uses
> its research and development money for operating
> capital, it loses its competitive edge because it no
> longer has the money needed to develop new products
> or to refine an existing product line. Thus when pri-
> vate philanthropy becomes maintenance money bail-
> ing out endangered institutions, it is no longer
> available to foster creativity and innovation. . . . It is
> likely to be insufficient as maintenance money, but it
> can be unusually effective as creative money.

For most of his career, Murray has occupied the unusual position of both fundraiser and grantmaker, as illus-

trated by his dual roles in the various challenge programs he has established. This gives him an opportunity to influence, in a subtle but profound way, the direction and ultimate character of many of these institutions. For the most part, he has been content to encourage simple gains in dollars and donors. But he also has been broadening his perspective to lead in ways that edge across the line from simple finance into philosophy. His recent tactic of encouraging specific kinds of voluntary support activity, such as strategic planning or contributions by young alumni, is illustrated by the emphasis he introduced in the Hospital Development Fund for 1991. Without fanfare, he set aside $150,000 to provide challenge grants for hospitals that wished to launch or improve health education programs with major campaigns.

This last item might easily be lost in the bigger picture. Why health education? The answer probably lies in Murray's understanding of the historic and special mission of Adventist health care that began with his days in public relations at CME. It probably also has a great deal to do with his creative and innovative response to a $500 "insult" from a company contributions committee in Fort Worth.

Murray condenses his thoughts on creativity into five key points:

> First, you must have a sense of urgency. For most of us, creativity flourishes best under pressure—pressure from ourselves or others. And it's a lot more pleasant when the pressure is self-induced. You must develop a conviction that what you are doing is just about the most important thing in the world. There will be times when you will say, "I don't know how I'm going to climb over this wall, but I simply *must* climb over it." With that attitude, your own natural creative process will show you how.
>
> Second, never be afraid to borrow someone else's good idea and adapt it to your situation. Nobody said that you have to be original, only that you have to be successful. But you still may need a large dose of pres-

sure-induced creativity to adapt that idea and make it successful in your organization.

Third, creative ideas in the philanthropic world by both donors and recipients can do much to affect the focus or direction of an institution and how it does business. Money talks. Use it creatively to inspire positive change.

Fourth, the benefits of creative ideas often are realized over the long haul. A good idea is like an elephant. It may have tremendous power, but it takes a while. There are relatively few brilliant program ideas in this business that have immediate payoffs. If you create a brilliant new program for your institution, or adapt someone else's, stay with it—and with that institution—long enough to make the idea work and be accepted. Many mediocre fundraising careers are littered with the refuse of creative programs that were aborted for lack of resolve.

And fifth, even though some people may naturally have a greater ability to solve problems, the creativity I'm talking about here isn't necessarily an inherent gift. As someone once said about good fortune, "The harder I work, the luckier I get." Creativity comes the same way, with hard work.

 7

The Value
of Persistence

The heights by great men reached and kept
Were not attained by sudden flight,
But they, while their companions slept,
Were toiling upward in the night.
> —*Henry Wadsworth*
> *Longfellow, "The Ladder*
> *of Saint Augustine,"*
> *stanza 10*

"I think it will happen someday."

As a general rule, Milton Murray is not used to failure. His career is strewn with successes, small and great. The paper ran the story. The donor said yes. The foundation accepted the proposal. The campaign reached its goal.

This is not to imply that he takes success for granted, relying recklessly on lucky stars or on that egocentric sense of destiny we tolerate only in genius generals or world leaders. Murray operates on exactly the opposite premise. He is an indefatigable detail man. His successes are produced by sweat, often slogged out in lonely hours spent staring at his portable typewriter in an economy-rate motel room far from home. He fights doggedly, and yet with a kind of cheerful abandon that says, "I'm simply doing my best." It is that whistle-while-he-works mentality that helps him keep his successes in perspective. When they occur, he is pleased and perhaps momentarily excited, but not really surprised. He may lose fervently fought battles but he inevitably wins the war. His faith in the ultimate efficacy of hard work is unwavering.

Unwavering, that is, until now. For nearly a decade, Murray has invested thousands of hours on a quest to persuade the U.S. Postal Service to issue a stamp honoring philanthropy in America. He has won countless battles. He wins them every day, whenever, through some complicated sequence of contacts, a high-powered senator or corporate executive is persuaded to write another letter to the postmaster general. But Murray has had to face the fact that all those successful battles have earned him extremely little apparent progress in actually winning the war. This is not the way it's supposed to be. Hard work, after a reasonable period of exercise, should be honored with success. Ten years is long beyond reasonable. And so, with a hint of puzzled exasperation infusing his matter-of-fact optimism, he says, simply: "I think it will happen someday."

Why this apparent infatuation with a stamp? Like the philanthropy calendar, the *Accent* publications, and his participation in the promotion of National Philanthropy Day, Murray has devoted a sizable portion of his professional career to causes and creations that raise consciousness as well as money. In Murray's view, fully credible philanthropy professionals must operate on three levels. The first level is the basic daily routine that ultimately raises money. The second involves those activities that help professionals do an even better job by learning new skills or helping others to do so through professional organizations. The third level requires professionals to help create the actual environment in which they work—that is, to help society understand and expand the role of philanthropy in maintaining the American way of life. That, of course, is where the calendar, the *Accent* publications, and National Philanthropy Day come in. And the stamp.

Murray has been a stamp collector ever since he was shamed into the hobby in a second-grade classroom. His family was on mission furlough back in the United States and for the first time in his life, seven-year-old Milton was mixing with a class full of American kids.

> One day the teacher asked if any of us collected stamps. Every hand in the room went up except mine. I already felt a little inferior because I was a missionary kid and hadn't quite caught up. When I got home that afternoon I went through the desks and the trash cans and found a few two-cent stamps. At Christmas my parents gave me a stamp book, and when we returned to South America a few months later my mother helped me. I'd bring out all the loose stamps I had collected and she would get down on the floor with me with a geography book and an atlas. We would go through my stamps and learn where each country was located and what its currency was. I learned a lot about the world as a direct result of collecting stamps.

It's more than fair to say that Murray has also learned a lot about the world as a direct result of campaigning for a stamp, for he was as naive when he started the second stamp enterprise as when he started the first. Although his own active campaign didn't begin until 1981, he had first considered the idea ten years earlier. At a meeting sponsored by AHP in Florida, Murray met John O. Newberry, chairman of the board of Community Service Bureau, a development and fundraising firm headquartered in Dallas, and president of a program called the Campaign for Philanthropy. Apparently they talked at some length about the need to raise the profile of philanthropy in American society, for Murray wrote in a follow-up letter:

> It was a pleasure to see you in Tampa and to again review the urgency for establishing a campaign in

behalf of philanthropy in our country. I am glad that
they have a man of your capability and standing in
the leadership role.

As I mentioned to you at the Happy Dolphin
Inn, there are two specifics that I have in mind that
should be part of the whole:

1. Why not work into the 1976 festivities by tying
    into Ben Franklin and other early fund raisers and
    have the national committee in charge of the bicen-
    tennial work in philanthropy to their program? In
    this connection maybe we should get the Postal
    Service to issue a stamp or a series of stamps point-
    ing to the concept of philanthropy. This should
    not be too difficult to sell since they are now issu-
    ing stamps for just about everything!

2. We should assign the various congressmen and sen-
    ators to individuals throughout the country to
    expose them to the necessity and values of the
    campaign we are talking about. I think that an
    outline of points to be covered with each of these
    representatives would be a guideline for each of us
    to follow. This must take high priority since Con-
    gress has such an impact on the country.

Today this letter and incident are loaded with irony.
Murray can only grimace at his naiveté when he reads the
line about a philanthropy stamp not being "too difficult to
sell." And the comment about Congress is even worse.
Hundreds of letters in his stamp file from senators and representatives prove that although Congress may have an impact
on the country, it has very little influence on the U.S. Postal
Service—at least when it comes to lobbying for something as
simple as a stamp.

Murray received an enthusiastic response from Newberry, but the U.S. Bicentennial came and went without Murray's hearing anything of substance about a campaign for
philanthropy or a new stamp. In the mid seventies, he talked

to the president of the American Association of Fund-Raising Counsel, who agreed to take up the idea with the leaders of the profession. Nothing came of it. By 1981 Murray was growing impatient and decided to take up the cause himself. After all, it shouldn't be "too difficult to sell."

Characteristically, Murray decided to start at the top, a technique he had learned from his army and college days. In this case, the top didn't mean the head of the Postal Service but the man who appointed the head of the Postal Service. Murray had no direct entrée to the Oval Office, but he had a close friend and mentor, Dan Benefiel, who was also a personal friend of the occupant of that office. In fact, Benefiel had been the young man who persuaded Ronald Reagan to enroll at Eureka College in Illinois in 1928. They had maintained their friendship ever since. Murray had known Benefiel for twenty years, since they worked together on a hospital campaign in Phoenix for the G. A. Brakeley Company.

Murray persuaded Benefiel to write to President Reagan about the stamp and Benefiel, through some connections of his own, was able to get the letter into the "family pouch" of personal mail for the First Family. Murray was delighted to learn of Benefiel's success, but when he received a copy of the letter Benefiel had written, he realized that something had slipped. The letter, warm and personal, yet succinct, asked Reagan to initiate procedures for a stamp honoring *voluntarism*, not philanthropy. Murray had goofed in prepping Benefiel properly and thus had bungled a great opportunity.

Murray heard nothing more of the results of Benefiel's letter, but he doubtless felt a pang of frustration when, in April 1983, the Postal Service issued the "Lend a Hand" stamp honoring voluntarism. Appreciative as he was of the "Lend a Hand" stamp, Murray also realized the sizable complication this now created for his own efforts. His imagination could already hear the patronizing answers: "But, Mr. Murray, I think we already did a stamp on being nice."

Murray was forced to turn his attention to a less dramatic and more mundane method: basic personal lobbying. In May 1982, he learned that Frank Pace, a personal acquaintance and chairman of the National Executive Service Corporation, had been appointed a member of President Reagan's newly established Task Force on Private Sector Initiatives. In the first of dozens of versions of the same message, Murray outlined his case for Pace and for the task force.

Reminding the task force of its own earlier action calling for corporations and individuals to double their philanthropic giving within four years, Murray claimed that a properly designed postage stamp could "bring philanthropy to the attention of America's entire population." He argued that nearly three billion pieces of first-class direct mail were sent by nonprofit organizations each year, reaching the equivalent of every man, woman, and child in America with one piece of nonprofit mail every four weeks. (Murray may have overestimated. In 1990, six years later, he used figures showing that nonprofit organizations sent eleven billion pieces of mail annually, with only 10 to 15 percent—one to two billion—going first class.) Further, he pointed out that although more than seventy specific philanthropic endeavors, including the Red Cross, the Salvation Army, and the Boy Scouts, had been honored by postal issues, the Postal Service had never once recognized philanthropy itself for its societal influence and its thoroughly American tradition. In addition, the nation's twenty million stamp collectors and their families made up nearly a fifth of the American population. In his ringing conclusion, Murray argued that to encourage the philanthropic spirit and achieve the goals of the presidential task force, "no other communication device would have such a deep penetration throughout America's society as would a postal issue." It was a bold claim, and however impressive it may have been to the task force, it was only another successful battle that had no discernible impact on the war.

The next eight years were more of the same, although Murray and the legions who eventually joined him in the cause maintained their courage by sharing stories of the lengthy campaigns for other stamps. A *Washington Post* article in 1986 told of a thirteen-year-old boy who proposed a George M. Cohan stamp and, years later, attended the issuing ceremony with his own grandchildren. A stamp honoring Haym Salomon, eighteenth-century philanthropist and financier of the American Revolution, was first proposed in 1931 and finally issued in 1975 as part of a Bicentennial series, which identified Salomon only as a "financial hero."

Murray quickly informed himself about the basic steps required to get a stamp approved. The typical procedure is for an idea to be recommended to the postmaster general by the Citizens' Stamp Advisory Committee (CSAC), a fourteen-member cross section of American society, most of whom have demonstrated some interest in philately. The committee meets every other month to recommend twenty-five to thirty issues a year out of two to three thousand proposals. The postmaster general has the authority to issue stamps without following CSAC's recommendations; however, for political reasons, this rarely occurs. An idea that has been rejected by CSAC can be brought back indefinitely for reconsideration simply by making a written request to the Postal Service.

Murray learned as much about lobbying and stamp politics as a dedicated amateur could probably be expected to ever know, and his techniques ranged from sophisticated subtlety to optimistic futility, from wooing the postmaster general to playing on even the remotest possibilities of public awareness. Perusing his well-thumbed stamp catalog one day he noticed that a stamp had been issued in 1954 honoring the 200th anniversary of Columbia University. Columbia is an important university, he thought. Perhaps influential people there would become excited about a philanthropy stamp. He wrote a letter to the editor of the university magazine, mentioning the Columbia stamp and his own efforts to establish one honoring philanthropy. The editor wrote back encouraging him to submit a short article about his campaign, using as background a history of the Columbia postal issue and others honoring higher education. However farfetched the chances were for meaningful results, Murray still invested the time to write a thousand-word piece. The article never appeared.

Murray also knew that he needed some impressive and tangible reminder, placed in the hands of selected leaders, to make his case in a succinct and attractive way. He prepared a "presentation book," bound in a gold-embossed, three-ring, rich leather binder. The looseleaf book, with each page inserted in a protective clear plastic sheet that allowed easy revision, contained carefully researched essays explaining the role of philanthropy in supporting the basic elements of American society, including education, hospitals, health care and research, youth, social welfare, arts and humanities, and other nonprofit enterprises. Murray illustrated each essay with postal issues through the years that had recognized different organizations or services in these areas.

With the presentation book as the first substantial weapon in his arsenal, Murray was eager to place copies in the hands of appropriate people. Dan Benefiel's letter to President Reagan hadn't achieved the desired result. Maybe the book would. Murray's challenge was to send the book to the president in a meaningful way that would attract his attention. Simply mailing it to the White House wouldn't do the trick; undoubtedly, the president received tons of material in that fashion. At that point in Murray's campaign he had no significant contacts in the White House. What one person, he wondered, within reasonable reach of his own professional station, could he become acquainted with who also had a legitimate reason to meet the president? *Eureka!* Murray contacted Dan Gilbert, the president of Ronald Reagan's, and Benefiel's, alma mater and enlisted his support. When Reagan visited the Eureka campus in February 1984, Gilbert presented him with Murray's book, explaining that Reagan's old friend and fellow Eureka alumnus Dan Benefiel was among the proponents of the idea.

In early 1984, Murray felt that things were going well. He had formed an ad hoc committee of some of the key leaders in the nonprofit world, including James Fisher of CASE, Robert Gale of the Association of Governing Boards, Landrum Bolling and Brian O'Connell of INDEPENDENT SECTOR, Barbara Marion of NSFRE, and Winthrop Wilson of AHP. In typical Murray fashion, he reported early and often on his persistent push for the stamp. A memo to the group in late February reported several items: (1) the apparent success at Eureka College; (2) an acquaintance with, and pledge of support from, Ursula Meese, wife of the attorney general, whom Murray had met at the First Day Issue ceremonies for the 1984 Love stamp; (3) a formal letter of request, drafted by Murray, from O'Connell to the postmaster general; and (4) the scheduling of appointments for Bolling to see the post-master general and key White House staffers. Murray also reported on his impending appointment with the head of the Postal Service Stamp Division, "to follow through at echelons below the Postmaster General," and on his own developing contacts at the White House. Still hopeful of securing First Family influence, he noted that he would also be "getting a friend on the West Coast to enlist the interest of a friend of the First Lady to forward a copy of the proposal to the White House with an endorsement." It was another long shot, but, to Murray's thinking, any shot was worth the effort.

Also typical of Murray's style was the sense of breathless immediacy of events, built on the perhaps feigned assumption that the stamp project occupied exactly the same position of urgency on the respective agendas of his supporting commit-tee members as it did on his own. He wrote, "As soon as this week concludes, even though I will be on the West Coast, I'll try to issue an update. If you have any suggestions or com-ments, feedback, etc., I'll be pleased to get it. To facilitate communications, my secretary will take your telephone mes-sage and relay it to me or ask me to call you. . . . I'll be back in my D.C. office on Tuesday, March 13, and will report back to you then or very soon thereafter."

Lest committee members lose their own sense of urgency by relying on Murray to do all the work, or forget their stake in the enterprise, he thanked them for their "enthusiastic support of this venture, which has only one purpose—to advance the cause of philanthropy and all the worthy efforts that gift dollars support year by year."

The next day Murray met with Donald M. McDowell, general manager of the Stamp Division of the U.S. Postal Service. McDowell affirmed the value of Murray's use of meaningful, specifically targeted influence, calling this the "rifle approach." He warned that Murray's cause might be hurt if the CSAC or postmaster general were harassed with a deluge of letters from John and Jane Doe before the idea had been formally considered. If and when the CSAC considered and rejected the philanthropy stamp proposal, McDowell counseled, a massive letter campaign might be appropriate.

Murray was a quick study. Throughout 1984 he planned and plotted, acknowledging each minor victory in modest memos to his colleagues and ignoring each defeat by diverting attention, his own and others', to new possibilities. He limited his efforts to McDowell's rifle approach, recruiting personal and professional acquaintances of CSAC members to write letters urging support for the stamp. He also took the bold step of meeting with a CSAC member directly. He learned that one of the CSAC members was a Hawaiian businessman and stamp collector named Ed Mallek. Murray was acquainted with a hospital in Hawaii and called an influential businessman who was a hospital board member. He asked the board member if he knew anyone named Ed Mallek. The board member did, and on Murray's request, he called Mallek, urging him to let Murray see him the next time Mallek was in Washington, D.C., for a CSAC meeting. Mallek agreed. When the two met, Murray made his case and was delighted with Mallek's suggestion that Murray write Mallek a personal letter outlining the proposal and send copies of the letter to all other CSAC members. Murray remembered McDowell's counsel about "harassing" the committee and wrote the letter only after receiving assurances from McDowell that this action shouldn't prejudice the committee or the USPS staff.

Murray knew that he had to make this letter stand out among the stacks of other letters received by the committee members. Murray already had the advantage that the letter was going out on Mallek's recommendation and thus should be received with more interest by the other members of the committee. Murray found other ways to make the letter count. His strategy with CSAC member "Digger" Phelps, head basketball coach at the University of Notre Dame, was typical. James Frick, long-time vice president at Notre Dame, was also a friend of Murray's. Murray asked Frick to give Phelps a friendly call, make a pitch for the stamp, and alert him to the forthcoming letter. Murray then asked Dick Wilson, president of NSFRE, to follow up with Phelps in writing, referring to Frick's conversation and forwarding the promised Mallek letter.

Murray used this "extended influence" technique often through succeeding years, and though the connections were sometimes tenuous, he never hesitated to pursue them. The decade saw four different postmasters general, and although each change meant lost influence, it also opened new possibilities for better connections. While attending a professional convention in 1986, Murray learned that John Brademas, then president of New York University, was a close friend of the recently installed postmaster general Preston Tisch. He also learned that Stephen Trachtenburg, president of the University of Hartford, was a close associate of Brademas. Through connections at CASE, he secured an appointment with Trachtenburg and persuaded him to work on Brademas, who in turn would work on Tisch. Similarly, in 1988, Murray asked a colleague at Hadley Memorial Hospital in Washington, D.C., who was on good terms with then Washington, D.C., mayor Marion Barry, to persuade His Honor to write to the postmaster general about the stamp.

These attempts assumed the effectiveness of the rifle approach, but as early as 1984, Murray realized that he must engineer greater pressure. In a September progress report to his ad hoc committee, he gave new meaning to the word *success* when he reported that, for the first time, the CSAC had formally considered the proposal for a philanthropy stamp. "Well," he wrote, "we have successfully negotiated another hurdle in the quest for a stamp featuring Voluntary Financial Support. On September 14 the Citizens' Stamp Advisory Committee declined to include the proposed stamp in the 1985 schedule in its formal recommendations to the post- · master general—however, we are all the more confident that it *will* happen. I am not endowed with prophetic talents and thus cannot hazard a date!"

Murray's consummate and nonchalant optimism must be credited for his ability to describe this apparent rejection as another hurdle "successfully negotiated." However, the failure forced him, in keeping with McDowell's earlier counsel, to suggest in that memo the launching of a full-scale, grassroots letter barrage on members of Congress, Postal Service officials, and big-league players in American business and philanthropy. He held off until the summer of 1986, when he began distributing thousands of promotional flyers to the philanthropy fraternity at professional conventions. At the same conventions, he set up booths where members could sign personalized, computer-generated letters to the members of Congress or U.S. Postal Service officials of their choice. He even asked development directors of the alma maters of U.S. representatives serving on the House Post Office and Civil Service Committee to write letters to their respective congressional alumni. He did the same with the alma maters of CSAC members.

On a whim, to test the possibilities for support, he introduced a petition at meetings of AHP and the National Catholic Development Conference, held a few days apart in California and Florida; he collected eight hundred signatures and mailed the petition to the postmaster general. In the cover letter he stressed that all the signers were people who made philanthropy happen in this country and thus fully understood its significance to national life. "So, Postmaster General Tisch," he wrote, "the will of the doers is that such a stamp be issued. If just one of us can bring together almost eight hundred signatures in less than ten working days, imagine the potential that is out there!"

However much these facts may have excited the postmaster general's imagination, he took no action, relying instead on the counsel of the CSAC, which steadfastly refused to recommend the philanthropy stamp. The primary objections, according to Murray's staff contacts in the Postal Service, related to design and profitability. Even accepting the awkwardness of trying to fit the word *philanthropy* on a postage stamp, is there any assurance that the general public knows what the word means? Philanthropy is an abstract concept. How do you effectively illustrate its fundamental societal role in one easily understood, universal image or symbol? Murray hired artists to come up with possible designs to help the committee overcome its fear. He readily acknowledged that the Postal Service never considers unsolicited designs, noting that he was supplying them merely as a starting point for discussion. His personal favorite was a vertical stamp with a single red rose on a stem, in front of a black background, with a reversed-out slogan reading "Giving Is Caring." Murray thinks that such a stamp has at least as much credibility and meaning for American society as, say, the highly sentimentalized 1986 "Love" stamp bearing the pop art image of a forlorn puppy.

But even if Murray had answered the design questions, he faced the bottom-line consideration: "Will it sell?" The Postal Service staff, charged with protecting the financial interests of the agency, kept this question before the committee and, according to Murray, doubtless influenced their enthusiasm for the idea. McDowell told Murray that the Postal Service tries to clear at least $5 million from every stamp it issues, which is the equivalent of selling twenty million first-class stamps beyond the break-even point. In the past, some stamps honoring specific philanthropic enterprises had not fared well, prejudicing key people against the future success of a general philanthropy stamp. Murray respectfully pointed out that the sales potential of *any* stamp honoring a specific and comparatively narrow philanthropic enterprise would be limited to those constituencies that were directly related to the enterprise. A "generic" philanthropy stamp, on the other hand, would be immediately attractive to almost *every* philanthropic, nonprofit entity in the country. To illustrate the point and to continue the pressure for the stamp, he quickly secured endorsements for the stamp from the national headquarters of thirty-four major groups, including the American Cancer Society, American Diabetes Association, American Heart Association,

American Red Cross, Boy Scouts of America, March of Dimes Birth Defects Foundation, Salvation Army, United Negro College Fund, United Way, and YMCA. It was an impressive list, representing, by example only, a huge and untapped potential resource for stamp sales. Murray even promised to raise money to promote the sale of the stamp through these and thousands of other organizations in the country. To date, his arguments have fallen on unresponsive ears. When asked how the CSAC or the Postal Service answers his arguments, he says, "By simply not producing the stamp."

While making his case on these fronts, Murray continued to foment his grass-roots letter-writing campaign. To its credit, the Postal Service is conscientious about answering letters; Murray has collected copies of hundreds of letters politely and noncommittally responding to the pleas or encouragement of U.S. senators and representatives; heads of corporations, major foundations, and philanthropic, humanitarian, and social welfare societies; professional organizations; and the general public. The petitioner's relative station or influence in American society has little or no effect on the content of the reply, but apparently does determine whether the barely personalized form letter will be signed by the postmaster general or another appropriate official.

Murray looked for any means to advance his cause. When fundraising consultant Jerold Panas presented Murray with a framed collection of stamps depicting nonprofit enterprises, Murray saw the immediate possibilities for his own campaign. Since then he has presented personalized, framed collections of stamps to White House chief of staff and stamp collector John Sununu, a postmaster general, an assistant postmaster general, and others. The stamps selected for the frame all relate in some way to a particular aspect of the recipient's career. In each case Murray finds some event to serve as the pretext for the presentation, such as a birthday or even, in the case of the postmaster general, the first anniversary of his installation in office. The presentation letter, however disinterested it may have begun, never ends without making a direct appeal for the philanthropy stamp.

Then there were the bookmarks. Murray made several thousand of them, each containing two or three colorful, philanthropy-related stamps on one side and a pitch for the philanthropy stamp on the other. It was a big job, for it required selecting and ordering large numbers of stamps from major suppliers, fabricating the inserts, applying the stamps, and cutting, sealing, and trimming the clear plastic lamination. As there was no budget for this campaign, Murray and a few volunteers did all the work by hand to keep the costs low. On cross-country flights, Murray often spread out the raw materials for several dozen bookmarks on the adjoining tray tables and empty seats, busying himself with several hours of cutting, sticking, and trimming. He distributed the bookmarks liberally, often using them as advance incentives to encourage hundreds of professional colleagues to write letters on behalf of the stamp. He also prepared custom-made bookmarks with stamps of specific interest to his lobbying targets.

> I attended a reception downtown for one of the several postmasters general we've had in the last few years. I had done the best I could to research his background and interests and those of his wife, and I found some stamps that illustrated these interests. I made up bookmarks for him and his wife with those stamps on the front and a message about the stamp campaign on the back. When I went through the receiving line I gave them to him and made my little speech about the stamp. Naturally, I hope he took those bookmarks home. I hope he gave his wife the bookmark I made for her and I hope she is a reader who will keep the bookmark in her books and look at it once in a while. And of course I hope she says to her husband, "Why don't you come out with a stamp for philanthropy?"

Hope, hope, hope. But hope that has been founded on years of work, work, work. Murray wins new high-level supporters at the White House, maintains close contact with U.S. Postal Service officials, and keeps an up-to-date address list of the CSAC, stretching his imagination for any idea, however tenuous or remote, that might bring the matter forcefully to the attention of the right influential person.

How does he keep it up? By this stage in his career, persistence is a Murray habit. Like hundreds of others laboring in the vineyards of philanthropy, he's seen it pay off too many times to sell it short now. Murray's professional experience has taught him that persistence is the bedrock of the business:

> In the early 1970s I worked with the campaign for the Shawnee Mission Medical Center in [Merriam,] Kansas. For forty-four months I sweated over, and submitted, four different proposals to the Kresge Foundation before receiving a $125,000 challenge grant. A few years earlier, during our campaign for Hackettstown Community Hospital in New Jersey, I had started wooing a nearby private foundation. In my view, the foundation *had* to give. It was part of the extended community to be served by the hospital. Therefore, as I saw things, it had a moral—if not a literal—obligation. The foundation, on the other hand, made it clear to us that it gave only to hospitals that were recognized by an appropriate accrediting body. At the time of my proposal the Hackettstown hospital was an empty lot. I continued poking and prodding with memos, news clippings, progress reports, and phone calls. Sixty months—a full five years—after my initial contact, the foundation awarded the hospital a $62,000 grant.
>
> Earlier, when I was in Phoenix, working for the G. A. Brakeley Company, I was assigned to a multi-hospital campaign. The campaign steering committee met to evaluate the giving ability of several prospective donors. When a certain Mr. Prospect's name came up, a pessimistic committee member withered expectations by declaring, "He's been in town for thirty years and has never done anything for the community."

A second committee member said, "Well, I think he might give $2,500 if he were approached in the right way," and another member thoroughly revived hopes when he added, "I met Mr. Prospect as he got off the train thirty years ago when his company in New York sent him out here. I know him fairly well. Although it's true that he hasn't done much, I think if he were asked in the right way, in due time he might be convinced to give $25,000."

Not surprisingly, the optimist was assigned as the campaign volunteer to cultivate Mr. Prospect; however, he needed the help of a campaign staffer. There I was, relatively new to the development business after leaving Loma Linda University. My associates figured this situation presented me with a good opportunity to learn about persistence and patience, so they assigned me to help the volunteer in his mission.

I started by going through my appointment calendar and writing in the volunteer's name every five or six weeks, as a reminder to communicate with him regularly on matters relating to Mr. Prospect. I quickly relayed any relevant news about the campaign to the volunteer to share with Mr. Prospect. I managed to keep up the flow of information, and the volunteer followed through famously on his end, orchestrating appropriate social occasions and gracefully sharing, over many months, information and ideas that might catch Mr. Prospect's interest.

A year and a half after the initial conversations, Mr. Prospect donated assets to the campaign that were immediately converted to $800,000 in cash.

I learned at least two lessons from this. The first was the importance of matching the right volunteer to the right donor. The results would probably have been much less impressive if either of the first two committee members had been assigned to cultivate Mr. Prospect. The second lesson, and one that I think I have learned well, is the value of patience and persistence in accomplishing anything visionary. In this instance, much of the time spent in making calls and sending notes and news clippings seemed little more than futile. After a year with no apparent glimmer of progress, it would have been easy to bail out and affirm the pessimistic prophecy of the first two committee members. But we stuck it out, the volunteer and I, and were richly rewarded for our persistence.

Murray credits his habitual persistence to an inspirational book published nearly forty years ago by one of his college professors. In the first chapter, titled "Too Soon to Quit," Harry Moyle Tippet (1951, p. 7) writes:

There is no discredit coming to a man who closes his life's endeavors in unfinished achievement if his face is toward the heights as his strength fails. The shame is due only him whose whole pathway is strewn with half-accomplished tasks or with the flukes of misadventure on the sea lanes of effort. Successful farmers do not leave their fields partly plowed in order to repair the highway. Masons do not stop building the foundations of a house in order to construct an outdoor fireplace. Shipbuilders who abandon a half finished warship in order to begin building a tugboat would be considered lacking in judgment. Yet many a worthy project has been lost to the world because somebody lacked vision to see it through, or someone else lost faith in its ultimate value, or yet another quit trying in the midst of his labors. . . . If there is anything the youth of today need to learn well, it is the truth that the quitter never wins and the winner never quits.

Murray has kept Tippet's book handy for years. The book, particularly the first and last chapters, has had such a profound influence on him that he secured permission from the publisher to reprint these chapters in pamphlet form. He has distributed hundreds of copies to young adults.

Is Murray any closer today to achieving his goal for a philanthropy stamp than he was in 1981 when he persuaded Dan Benefiel to write a personal appeal to his friend Ronald Reagan? It is hard to say, but Murray insists that he won't give up. At the same time, he is beginning to worry about the percentage of his recent professional life that he has devoted to the cause and whether, conscientiously, he can continue, when he is paid to do other work. Had he no other callings in life right now, he would retire and devote his full attention to the campaign for the stamp, hoping, as always, to see the dream fulfilled.

"I think it will happen someday."

 8

The Effectiveness
of Anonymity

Men with a passion for anonymity.
—*Franklin Delano Roosevelt,*
Report of President's
Committee on Administrative
Management, Jan. 12, 1937

Emily Dickinson, the nineteenth-century Amherst recluse and
poet, once wrote:

I'm nobody! Who are you?
Are you nobody, too?
Then there's a pair of us—don't tell!
They'd banish us, you know.

How dreary to be somebody!
How public, like a frog,
To tell your name the livelong day
To an admiring bog!

Note: The Dickinson poem is reprinted by permission of the publishers and
the Trustees of Amherst College from THE POEMS OF EMILY DICKIN-
SON, Thomas H. Johnson, ed., Cambridge, Mass.: The Belknap Press of
Harvard University Press, Copyright 1951, © 1955, 1979, 1983 by the President and Fellows of Harvard College.

140

For the most part, Milton Murray has lived the professional life of Dickinson's poem, although he probably finds the ideal more succinctly phrased by fundraising oracle Harold J. Seymour (1988, p. 183) in his dictum: "Blending yourself quietly into the background, at any rate, is a good rule to start with." Seymour's counsel, penned fifteen years after Murray began his career in public relations and philanthropy, was aimed at "newcomers and trainees." Twenty-five years later, Murray still lives by it.

This may seem an ironic or even dubious claim for a man whose penchant for anonymity hasn't slowed the steady stream of awards and honors conferred on him, including the Harold J. Seymour Award from AHP and the Outstanding Fund-Raising Executive of the Year Award from NSFRE, or tempered his enthusiasm for the writing of this book. In Murray's view, however, his professional mannerism of "blending quietly into the background" has been the primary factor in his accomplishment of things worth writing about.

An incident in the $3.3 million campaign for Huguley Hospital in Fort Worth, Texas, in the 1970s illustrates Murray's customary practice of self-effacing anonymity to accomplish his purposes.

When we did the feasibility study for Huguley, we had figured on getting about $750,000 from each of the two major foundations in the city. My whole idea for the campaign was built on that premise, and I had agreed to be involved on that assumption. At an early meeting of the campaign steering committee, one of the suits across the table—we'll call him Mr. Pessimist—said, "You know, you're not going to get more than $300,000 combined out of those foundations."

He might as well have said that I was a jewel thief, considering the potential impact his remark could have on my credibility, on the expectations of the committee, and on campaign morale. On the surface, it was a direct challenge to the most basic premise of the meeting, which was no inconsequential bit of sweatshop chatter during coffee break. We had some heavy-hitting Fort Worth community and business leaders in that room, giving their time to this enterprise. A torpedo like that could sink the whole project.

Naturally, I felt put on the spot. The collective gaze of everyone in the room zeroed in on me, waiting for a response. I had to make a quick decision. If I admitted that Mr. Pessimist was right, I effectively killed the campaign. On the other hand, I felt it risky to dispute his opinion in front of his peers, so I simply said, "Oh, is that right? I had thought otherwise," and changed the subject.

Why did I do that? Because I remembered in the nick of time that I wasn't the leader of this campaign. I was the staffer. It's the campaign leader's job to lead and the staffer's to support and coordinate. However, this is sometimes a very easy thing to forget. After all, the campaign's volunteer leaders are heavily—sometimes even totally—dependent on the staffer's expertise and guidance. In this case, if I had contradicted the pessimist, I would have focused attention on myself as having leadership authority instead of relying on the volunteers, who could provide it much more effectively than I could. Ego being what it is, a challenge to the premise of the campaign could all too easily become a personal challenge that would be difficult to ignore. But these challenges often must be ignored, deflected onto the leadership, or handled in a less public way.

Why? Because Mr. Pessimist has an ego of his own. He was on the committee because he is a person of distinction and influence in the community. The chances are good that he didn't get there without a fairly high regard for his own opinions. Like the rest of us, he doesn't like to see them challenged. He likes to feel important and the moment I contest his judgment, I threaten him and depreciate him before his peers.

At the same time, I had to do *something* to counter the potential devastation of his pessimism. So, in this incident, I let the remark go undisputed in the meeting, but when the meeting ended I headed straight for the office of another committee member who hadn't been present and who carried considerable influence with his peers. I told Mr. Influence what Mr. Pessimist had said, and I reminded him that if Mr. Pessimist was right in reducing our expectations about the two foundations, we ought to call the whole campaign off right then. We needed at least $1.5 million. Mr. Influence agreed.

I made sure Mr. Influence was at the next meeting and that he was able to make a few offhand remarks reiterating that we needed $1.5 million from the foundations or we wouldn't succeed. That's all it took. The committee quietly and politely forgot Mr. Pessimist's discouraging words and proceeded according to my original strategy.

And we got $1.5 million from the foundations.

I believe that we were successful because the committee's collective will to go after the money had been preserved without an embarrassing debate. A debate might have made me feel like "somebody" on the committee for the moment, but it would have skewed my proper relationship to the volunteers. I preempted that debate by suppressing my ego and applying Seymour's good advice about blending quietly into the background.

Murray began his quest for professional anonymity during his years building a public relations office at the College of Medical Evangelists (now Loma Linda University) in Loma Linda, California. He started as a one-person department. When he left eleven years later, he supervised seventeen full-time employees in publications, community relations, and development. Often the instigator behind newsworthy happenings, Murray nevertheless instructed his subordinates to keep his name out of news releases and his face out of photographs. Ignoring the ego-gratifying potential for an institutional spokesman or press secretary to become a community personality in his own right, Murray assiduously conceived and orchestrated events and pronouncements in the name of other campus administrators. He explains that he also deliberately limited how much he allowed himself to be seen with the top brass.

> The public relations function was new at Loma Linda and did not have the stature to warrant a vice presidency. Yet the president knew that it was important, so I had good access to him. However, I didn't like to exploit that access publicly, because I believed that it would hurt my credibility with my colleagues whose public relations consciousness I wanted to raise.
>
> In those days, the president had a fairly high personal profile on campus. He'd often eat in the cafeteria with other administrators. I made it a matter of policy never to eat with him there or to be seen by other employees huddling with him about this or that.
>
> I wanted my colleagues to value PR on its own merits and not just because I had the president's ear. I wanted them to respond to my requests or encouragement because they respected me as a professional and not because they thought I had influence with the big shots. If I were perceived as a kind of "bodyguard" to the president, I would lose my touch for getting things done at the grass-roots level for the employees, their departments, and the whole institution. Naturally, I wanted to have influence with the president. I just didn't want people to think I had it. If they did, they'd respond to me for political reasons instead of professional ones. I didn't want that.

Murray also was fussy about his job title, again for philosophical reasons. As a neophyte officer in public relations who was hoping to convince his colleagues of its importance, he nevertheless refused apparent good-faith attempts by the administration to give his office the very credibility he craved for it. In the Loma Linda milieu, as in many institutions today, the term "director" implied a level and degree of administrative responsibility and prestige that was securely within the range of middle management. When the administration offered to upgrade Murray's title to director of public relations, and later to director of public relations and development, he demurred. To the puzzlement of his superiors, he requested the title of "coordinator," a term that generally carried much less respectability in the subtle insinuations of academic semantics.

Words are important, so it is interesting to see how we sometimes use them in strange ways without reference to their real meaning. Many institutions arbitrarily decide that "coordinator" is less prestigious than "director," though the words themselves imply no such thing. As generally understood by the real world outside the quadrangle, they have an apple-and-orange relationship that logically accepts no ranking. It is perhaps universally understood that 4 is "greater" than 3. Not so with "director" and "coordinator." Of course, we in fundraising do the same thing, with much less uniformity, as indicated by our donor walls and giving clubs. One university's "patron" is another's "supporter," and one hospital's "sponsor" is another's "pacesetter." These are all artificial euphemisms that serve an expedient purpose in academia and philanthropy. However, I didn't care about euphemisms and their implied pecking order. I was content with a term that actually described the nature of my work, or rather, my philosophy of the nature of my work, regardless of its status. That's why I wanted to be called coordinator instead of director.

Directors *direct*. "Do this." "Do that." People not under a director's supervision can say to him: "Hey, don't trouble me. That's your problem. You're the director. You're *It*." Well, I didn't like being *It*.

On the other hand, coordinators *coordinate.*
This idea describes equal members of a group working toward a common goal. The coordinator merely
helps the other members of the group to be efficient
in their progress. I liked that model, because it
described exactly what I was trying to accomplish at
Loma Linda. I wanted all the employees in the college, not just my subordinates, to understand what
public relations was about and to do their part for the
institutional image as shareholders in a common mission. I was there to "coordinate" *their* efforts. I suppose the administrators thought that I was a little
naive in my purist insistence on philosophical semantics at the expense of in-house respectability, but they
let me have my way.

Today, of course, the situation is different. I
think there now is a legitimate place for a "director"
and a "vice president." In the sense that a director
today often "directs" a large staff of workers who are
immediately responsible to that director, the term has
merit. But I believe that true advancement professionals in public relations or development should be more
interested in coordinating the advancement consciousness of all of the employees, not only those who show
up in the advancement column of the institutional
flow chart.

Even today, in smaller nonprofit organizations,
great damage can be done to the credibility of public
relations and philanthropy if we create fancy titles
and lots of column inches in the in-house newsletter
before people really understand and appreciate what
we are doing. Why? Because in some settings there is
already a lot of unfortunate but deserved skepticism
about those hot-shots over in PR and fundraising.
Consider education, for example. Faculties are noto-
rious for the jaundiced eye with which they view
advancement activities. They rightly snicker at the
shallow, hollow claims made in glossy recruitment

viewbooks and videos. And they are provoked by shameless attempts to lure big gifts with honorary doctorates—but only when it's for the other guy's department.

Your institution is probably different. Your recruitment materials are credible and your honorary doctorates well deserved. But you can count on the fact that many of your faculty will believe otherwise. That's just the nature of how things work in the quadrangle. In that semi-hostile context, it probably will hurt you as an advancement professional to become a big name on campus too soon. To develop substance and credibility with your peers, you must prove yourself in low-profile ways. That often happens by painstakingly winning the confidence of the faculty, one department—or even one professor—at a time. It probably won't help much to have your grip-and-grin photo in the paper receiving a fat check from a local corporation. That's the president's job, not yours.

Of course, there is a price to pay. Murray's relentless low-profile approach has annoying side effects. Many people in his organization, even influential ones, still do not understand and therefore do not respect or credit the work of his offices.

Examples of collegial indifference usually provoke a reaction. His subordinates enjoyed Murray's good-natured but pointed outburst in a staff meeting a few days after the Adventist worldwide quinquennial business session in Indianapolis, Indiana, in July 1990. Murray reported that President George Bush had sent a letter of congratulation at the opening of the session. The letter noted that American religion has made "valuable contributions in philanthropy, education and the arts" and praised Adventists for "sponsoring charitable programs world-wide, particularly in the fields of education, health care and emergency relief." Murray was delighted that the president's statement referred directly to philanthropy and charitable giving. He was irritated, however, with the church's own brief mention of the letter in the general church news magazine covering the session. The one-sentence news summary ignored Bush's reference to "philanthropy" and "charitable programs," both key words in Murray's lexicon because they assume the actual act of giving private money. The report said simply that Bush praised Adventists "for their *work* [emphasis added] in education, health care and emergency relief."

The distinction may seem extremely slight to the uninitiated layperson, but to Murray it makes a big difference. A great opportunity was lost, he thundered, to remind church members of the value of giving money to worthy causes. While that concept might be vaguely included in a reference to Adventist "work," why muddle it up when the president of the United States himself had put it in such clear, specific terms? If the "work" that won presidential approbation is to continue and grow, members must be reminded—with specific language—to "give money."

Murray's philosophy of essential anonymity ignores a basic principle long understood in politics, advertising, and even religion: personalities promote causes. The function must have form and in many instances, particularly with new ideas, the easiest and most efficient form is a face, a voice, a "style." Murray has studiously refused to give his function the form of his personality.

He hates committee meetings and absents himself whenever possible from all in-house political discussion not directly related to his specific domain. This is somewhat unusual in an organization where achievement of a certain level of administrative stature in one department, which Murray possesses, tacitly qualifies one to speculate authoritatively on the business of another.

In addition, for most of his career, he generally avoided those genteel social occasions where the personality shines while business is subtly transacted. He never learned to play golf, deciding that he could accomplish more at his desk than on the green, though in his later years his opinion on that point has begun to modify. "If I had it to do over again, I'd probably play golf. I see the value of it now," he says.

Throughout his career Murray has refined, as does any good philanthropy professional, the skill of giving other people credit for his good ideas and achievements. For him, that is the second best work of the philanthropic professional. The best work is encouraging and training others, particularly his colleagues and superior executives, to develop good ideas and achievements on their own. This process usually begins by sharing credit for his work with them. It inspires in them a sense of ownership, and ownership of the enterprise, Murray maintains, is the key to advancing philanthropy. "If I promoted philanthropy in my organization by exploiting my personality, with lots of glitz and handshaking and my picture in the paper, what happens when I am gone? Philanthropy fizzles. 'Oh, that. That was Murray's hobbyhorse, nobody else's.' But if I promote it quietly, by patiently and painstakingly securing the executives' intellectual ownership of this enterprise, philanthropy will continue to flourish on its own. It becomes their collective hobbyhorse, and, thereby, the whole organization's. That's what I work for."

In 1990, a brief news item in the church news magazine caught Murray's attention. It said that an ad hoc organization was raising money from American churches for an interfaith chapel at Camp David. Murray thought his organization ought to participate. Through his church's military chaplain's office, Murray learned that the campaign was founded and headed by Kenneth H. Plummer, Sr., a Methodist layperson and retired building contractor from Chambersburg, Pennsylvania, who had previously built some of the buildings at the camp.

Murray called Plummer on September 8 and asked for details. Plummer explained that the campaign goal was set at $1 million. To ensure a multifaith representation in the financial support base, the campaign limited single gifts to $100,000, with a maximum of $300,000 from any one of the five major world religions—Judaism, Hinduism, Islam, Buddhism, and Christianity.

Murray had to know the size of a reasonable gift; he hesitated to quote a figure. Emphasizing that he was not an officer or decision maker, he finally suggested that he could work for a $25,000 gift. Plummer thought that would be respectable.

When the conversation ended, Murray immediately switched roles from potential donor to fundraiser. Where would he get $25,000, and on short notice? He wanted the check to be presented at the annual Dinner for Philanthropy he was to host for church leaders on October 4, just twenty-six days later. He had to work fast.

He decided that he could put up $2,000 from his philanthropy calendar reserve fund. That would convince church leaders that he was serious. He called a favorite major donor and briefly described the project, noting the public relations value of the church's participation. He asked, "If the church could come up with $7,000, would you consider underwriting a third of the remainder—$6,000?" The donor tentatively agreed. That's all Murray needed.

He met with church officials and said, "We can participate in this worthy project for $25,000. However, I have reason to believe that I can find three donors who will give $6,000 each if the church comes up with the remaining $7,000, and I can take care of $2,000 of that. What do you think?"

The officials saw that for $5,000, the church would be credited with a $25,000 gift, or one-twelfth of the Christian financial representation in the project. With their approval, Murray reported back to the donor, who confirmed his tentative commitment. Then Murray called up two other donors and asked them to split the remaining $12,000. With so much momentum behind the project, they found it easy to agree.

October 4 came. Murray wrote the presentation letter. It read:

Dear Mr. Plummer:

It is with a distinct sense of pleasure that we share the enclosed check for $25,000 written out to the Camp David Chapel Fund. This comes to you from your friends and Christian colleagues in the Seventh-day Adventist Church. . . .

May the blessings of our Lord be bountiful as the Chapel contributes to the spiritual well-being of those who worship there from week to week.

The letter was signed, not by Murray, but by the president of the Seventh-day Adventist Church, Robert Folkenberg.

When Folkenberg made the speech and presented the check to Plummer—accompanied by a hearty ovation from the banquet guests—nobody was looking at Milton Murray. And that's just the way he wanted it. His simple philosophy of anonymity explains why.

First, remember who you are not. You are not the president, but the fundraiser. You are not the campaign leader, but the staffer. When you forget who you are not, you're in trouble.

Second, it is more important to earn respect for your work than for yourself. Philanthropic fundraising is a profession whose driving force is altruistic love. That most noble form of love is expressed in a willingness to put someone or something else before yourself. It will be hard to be a success in philanthropic fundraising when you put yourself before your work.

Third, respect for your work will not necessarily come with your job title, with your public access to the president or high society, or with the frequent appearance of your picture in the paper. Respect for your work will come when you convince others to join you in doing it.

Some sage once observed that a person can go anywhere and do anything as long as he doesn't have to get the credit for it. Philanthropy professionals like Murray prove this proverb daily. Much of the creativity and detail work in philanthropic enterprises must be handled by those who are willing to blend themselves quietly into the background, content to see their key role go unacknowledged in the news story and the apparent credit go somewhere else at the annual banquet. They do not depend on public affirmation or acclaim for job satisfaction. They don't seek the ego stroking that is sometimes disguised more respectably as "feedback." They like the work for its own sake, and they selflessly love their cause.

At a staff meeting one day, his young subordinates laughed at the punchline of a typical Murray peroration. Two of them reached for pen and paper to record it word for word.

"I've trained myself to *enjoy* doing the work, simply because it needs to be done," Murray roared, *"and phooey on the feedback!"*

 9

Loyalty and Commitment: Keys to the Giving Life

The greatest rewards come only from the greatest commitment.

—Arlene Blum, as quoted in
Kouzes and Posner, 1987,
p. 279

When he was thirty-nine years old, Milton Murray distressed many of his friends and made his mother cry.

He left the work.

"Left the work." It's an odd phrase, largely unintelligible, in its full significance, to the uninitiated. Yet to thousands, even hundreds of thousands, of people in one of Milton Murray's worlds, it is a phrase fraught with foreboding. In Murray's case, the idea of his leaving was particularly disconcerting because those who knew him well firmly believed that Murray, of all people, was rock solid on the philosophy of staying. And indeed, he still was. Nevertheless, he left.

By 1961 Murray had worked in public relations and development at the College of Medical Evangelists for almost twelve years. He was disappointed and restless. Although administrators of the college praised him occasionally for his good work in building a new administrative function from scratch, he wondered if public relations and development would ever be fully recognized as a legitimate, even vital, part of the institutional machinery. In his view, the institutional process of accepting change moved agonizingly slowly. The sweat-work and requisite patience of genuine, long-term philanthropic enterprise that he assiduously advocated seemed to be repeatedly ignored for the allure of glittering "easy money" fundraising schemes. In Murray's view, CME, like a surprising number of similar organizations, paid little mind to cultivating friends and yet expected to find lots of them when it came time to make the big ask. The institution was not forming the kind of professional fundraising program that would generate a solid flow of voluntary financial support.

Harold Shryock, associate dean of the medical school in the early fifties and one of Murray's administrative mentors, recalls some of CME's views about fundraising at the time:

> During those years, one of our business managers was a man who had come up through the ranks in the institution. He started out as a young man driving the truck to pick up the trash and eventually became comptroller—the ranking business manager. His concept of how to balance a budget was homegrown. To get money, you went to somebody who had some and you begged for it. Your appeal was that you needed it for a specific purpose. You didn't think of endowments; you spent the money as fast as you got it. This man hoped that W. K. Kellogg would someday release funds that would help us balance our budget, but I don't think much came of this idea.
>
> Sometime during that period, the school hired a man to solicit funds. He would go around trying to get widows to give a few hundred dollars. That's the way it was done in those days.

Milton had other ideas. He and the administration didn't sing off the same page. In his early days at CME, when he was still focused primarily on public relations and was just beginning to think about fundraising, he came to me one day and said, "The brethren tell me they're not satisfied with my way of doing things. Should I stick it out or not?" I asked him if he was convinced that he knew how it should be done. When he said yes, I told him, "Stay with it. Even if they don't recognize that you've got something worthwhile, if you're convinced, you'll be successful in some other context."

Murray began thinking seriously of "other contexts" in the late fifties. In 1960 the trustees appointed a vice president to be in charge of certain fundraising activities. Murray was pleased that his own fledgling development operation would remain independent and unaffected by the new appointment, but he felt that the trustees' action amounted to a vote of no confidence for his ideas about voluntary financial support. In Murray's view, the new vice president offered no hope for long-range professionalism in advancement. His career had been focused in education and the ministry, with little evidence of interest in or commitment to philanthropic fundraising. When would they ever learn?

Murray decided that he had to make a foray into the real world of philanthropy and show what could be accomplished. His organization's huge humanitarian operations, he reasoned, would not understand the range of realistic funding possibilities, already exploited in the postwar era by American higher education and health care institutions, unless an Adventist actually went out, learned the business as a true professional, and returned with convincing successes on a résumé. So he decided to "leave the work."

In 1960 Adventist parlance, being in the work meant being on the church payroll in any of more than 40,000 blue- or white-collar jobs (by 1988 the number was 115,000) in the organization's global enterprises in education, health care, publishing, humanitarian aid, health food manufacturing, the ministry, and general administration. The denominational colleges had been founded decades earlier on the premise that the majority of their graduates would enter the work and dedicate their professional lives to the advancement of the church's mission, usually at sacrificial "missionary" wages. For thoroughly dedicated first- or second-generation Adventist workers, like Murray's parents, it could be discomfiting, if not heartrending, when children they sent through the church's schools chose to work "outside." Even if higher salaries (Murray's would nearly double) and—as they viewed it—the potentially questionable attractions and associations of the everyday secular world did not take their inevitable toll on fervent Christian commitment, it was still a waste of talent and expertise that could more efficiently advance the work.

From the moment Murray's professional eye began to wander, he vigorously asserted his firm loyalty to churchwork. He argued that his only interest in leaving was to better qualify himself for his ultimate return with the credentials necessary to convince skeptical church leaders.

In a mimeographed memo to his colleagues late in 1960, he officially informed them of his plans and flatly asserted, "I don't want this to be construed that I am withdrawing from denominational work. I am not."

His mother, doubtless convinced of her son's honorable intentions, nevertheless questioned his resolve to follow through. She cried. Thirty years later, LaDelle Phillips, more than ninety years old and a lifelong friend from the senior Murrays' days in South America, recalled: "Golda Murray came to visit me and told me about Milton's plans. We both wept that day. We thought that if Milton left the work, he would never come back."

Murray's friend Harold Shryock agrees. "I feared that his plans would take him permanently out of the denominational ranks—not in terms of membership, but in terms of what he could offer in productivity. I heard his promise that he was just leaving for experience, but I've seen other people make the same promise and not follow through. I was afraid that he'd weaken on that promise."

Milton's father, Walter Murray, was by this time one of three vice presidents at the church's worldwide headquarters, then located in Washington, D.C. His long years of administrative experience had taught him many lessons about the fate of progressive ideas in the battle against corporate mentality. Milton had kept his father informed of some of his frustrations at Loma Linda, factors that doubtless added a political aspect to a career "project" that was otherwise inspired by altruistic motives. Although the elder Murray apparently shared little of his wife's or Shryock's concern about Milton's venture, he used the occasion to write his son a cautionary and fatherly epistle about patience and loyalty to the organization.

Dear Milton:

In beginning let me say that in a certain sense it is fortunate for your project that [a vice president] has been appointed to the work of soliciting. There was one thing I feared when you talked to me about your project and that was that the organization at CME would think you were unfair with them to ask to be released when they might be left without the proper help in PR when you left. One should not take advantage of his employer when the employer "is over the barrel." I realize that there is something in humanity that sometimes indicates this, either from indifference to the employer's needs or to the passion of the employee. . . . In my own thinking it is unethical to do this in a Christian organization. Now, CME will have a man to at least take some care of the job you leave, if they desire.

You have given me the idea that you think the Trustees have not been following your lead in PR. As an onlooker, with some knowledge of the things that have gone on, I think that you have been able to carry on a program with success quite a bit above the average. I think you have been patient with the Trustees and I think that pretty generally they have followed as closely as they could be expected to the program you have put before them. I have sometimes marveled at the confidence the administration has had in you. It is not easy to begin as you did rather new in the field and be able to forge such a well-balanced program of PR when this branch of our organization is so new. I personally have had to introduce projects to boards, constituencies, etc., for some twenty-seven years and from my experience and observation I think what you have done through the years would merit a pretty good batting average. Of course, I understand you might have wished and wanted to get going faster, but you know it is dangerous for any soldier to get too far ahead of his regiment.

As you carry on from here you will be extra wise to be just as considerate as possible of CME in making the adjustment into the new setup, whatever that may be. You will be well advised to take the attitude that your job belongs to the organization, and the staff is also of the organization. Some on your staff will look at this new [vice presidency] as an injustice to you. Some will think that they are advancing [this man] ahead of you who have put in so many years at CME. I do not think the Trustees had this in mind, but they evidently thought of enlarging the personnel so that more progress could be made. . . . I have to remember that the organization has paid me for the work I have done, and the job I have held is the organization's to give to whomsoever they will. One of the ways men are led to appreciate other men is to see themselves denied of their services. Many boards have only seen a worker's value when they have been denied of his services. In this case we cannot say what will be the board's evaluation of your service. That must always be decided by time. . . .

This is a time you will have to exercise extra faith in the sincere intentions of your fellow men in the organization. . . . The members on our boards are sincerely seeking some way to solve, to the best of their ability, the problems before them. Sometimes there may be some ulterior motive in somebody's mind, but there is a guiding Hand, the Hand of God, that will make these things right in His own good time. . . .

I am glad that you have made it clear that your life purpose is to serve the Church. Stick to that. Take it from one who was yesterday sixty-six years old that this is the best way. I have had times when I thought that the brethren did things which were to my disfavor, but now as I see things with the perspective of time, I am satisfied to have had them the way they happened. Man is born to trouble. We must learn to set our sails so that we can even sail against the wind. Remember in all this, that God looks down on us as a Merciful Heavenly Father and He will not suffer us to be tried above that which we are able [to bear] by the help of His grace.

There will be people on your staff who will be feeling sorry for you. Others will maybe take your side and try to work up sentiment in favor of you. I have sometimes been led away with this kind of procedure in my younger days, but just remember this: that the people on your staff may have a loyalty to you, but they have a greater loyalty to the Church and there are not very many in our world who are willing to get out on a limb for another and stay there till the limb is sawed off. I have had people take my part very earnestly when they talked to me, but when it came to a showdown in the time I needed help, they thought otherwise. You must not think badly of humanity for this. Humanity is made that way. That's the kind of world we live in. There are some battles we have to fight alone. Keep up your courage, even if you think you have lost a battle (I think you have not). Remember you are a long ways from losing the war. . . .

Lovingly yours,

Daddy

Loyalty became a Murray watchword, and he stuck with his plan. He engineered a leave of absence, beginning in February 1961, and started work with the G. A. Brakeley Company at its Phoenix, Arizona, office, where he committed himself to a minimum two-year assignment. In September, in a mimeographed letter to his colleagues in Loma Linda, he acknowledged that after six months in his new work his "CME experience has contributed more to Phoenix than Phoenix will have contributed to CME. The programming here is such that as of November 1 I will be getting more and more into the thick of fundraising, writing basic presentations and obtaining the type of experience that I set out to get."

During those six months, CME administrators accepted a report from a John Price Jones study regarding the institution's development potential. In a memo to his staff at CME, Murray noted that "among many other good recommendations, [the report] advises the College to gear up its development offices immediately with good leadership. I can only concur with this recommendation and although I must admit that I could have hoped that the administrators and trustees would have sensed the importance in years gone by, I'll be happy if they do so now."

Murray told his staff that he had advised the college to go ahead and find a replacement and not to wait for his return, because, he wrote, he had "made it quite plain to the president that I am presently bent on getting the experience I want and that the institution should not consider me for any capacity."

In an honorable lame-duck call for unity, Murray counseled his young and disappointed staff: "Please be helpful and sympathetic with whomever the trustees give the responsibility to direct development affairs. Such a person will need the help more than anything else. You can continue to show your esteem for me by . . . good staff work. Above all, be loyal.''

In Phoenix, Brakeley had contracted to run a campaign for the Miracopa County Hospital Development Association, a consortium of five hospitals in the metropolitan area. Murray's superiors tapped him to be in charge of the communications and community relations portion of the campaign. Public relations staffers from each of the hospitals reported to Murray once a month for general briefings on the campaign and specific direction for their involvement.

For the first few months Murray fidgeted. The job seemed to be a throwback to the eight or nine years when he pounded out his own news releases at Loma Linda. He worked at his usual pace and found the workload uncomfortably light. When would he start learning about real fundraising?

Yes, I went to Brakeley to learn about fundraising, and yes, six months later I still wrote news releases. But I had to be fair to the company. They didn't bring me there as a development intern or trainee. They brought me there to work. So I hadn't the slightest cause to complain when they assigned me to the place where I would make the greatest contribution, even if it was a yawner for me.

Fortunately, that only lasted about six months. Dan Benefiel, a long-time pro who had himself recently joined Brakeley to head up the Phoenix campaign, called me in one day. He said, "Milt! You ought to become a fundraiser"—as though the thought had never occurred to me. "I want to put you in charge of the employee giving program for this campaign. You're going to help them raise $600,000."

Officials from several of the big employers in town, including the Motorola plant, were on the campaign board. So it was natural for us to expect their companies to help us with a campaign among their employees. Dan helped me get started with Motorola, working through their personnel department. From there on, it was all new and exciting and I learned fast. Motorola was my pilot project, in which we raised the first $70,000 of our employee campaign goal. With that experience behind me, I started campaigns at several other companies simultaneously. And after that I worked on getting the physicians to raise $700,000.

After Phoenix, Brakeley took Murray to the Los Angeles area for a series of campaign feasibility studies. In 1964, through a complex set of events and networking contacts, Murray accepted an invitation from the University of Southern California and the Ford Foundation to establish a development program at the Autonomous University of Guadalajara—the first such program in a private university in Latin America. The three years spent there (discussed in more detail in Chapter Four) provided Murray with many opportunities for international consulting and raised his standing even higher in the fundraising fraternity. The transition from Brakeley to Guadalajara gave Murray an opportunity to test his definition of loyalty in broader ways. When the Ford Foundation officials agreed to help establish a development program at Guadalajara, they commissioned Thomas Nickell, vice president for development at USC, to find someone for the job. Nickell, who had known Murray as a professional colleague during Murray's Loma Linda days, asked him to consider the job. Intrigued by the idea, Murray nevertheless decided to be frank about his Sabbath observances.

I told him that I wouldn't be able to work on Friday nights or Saturdays and explained that the difficulties in getting others to understand that, particularly in a different culture, might be insurmountable. He asked if I could get some kind of dispensation. I explained that my church doesn't work that way. Members are responsible for their own actions and will finally answer for them, individually, regardless of what others may have encouraged or condoned. I said, "We take this as a directive from the Holy Scriptures." He didn't seem very pleased.

A couple of days later he discovered that I could speak Spanish. I guess that made my candidacy all the more attractive in his eyes—enough, at least, to make him want to work around my stubbornness on the Sabbath question. He asked if I would at least go talk to the people at Guadalajara. I agreed. He said, "Now I don't want you to bring up anything about your Sabbath." I assured him that I wouldn't, but that I wouldn't take the job without my position being fully understood. He said, "We'll talk about it when you get back."

Things went well on my visit. Ten days after I returned from Mexico, the university president from Guadalajara, Luis Garibay, met with Tom and me at USC. Tom said, "I guess I'm here to perform a marriage. But before I do there is one point I must mention. Milton will not work on Saturdays."

Garibay just smiled. "No problem. We know Adventists. We have a lot of Adventists in our medical school, and they don't study or go to class on Saturday. In fact, we like them because they are serious students. We'll take Murray."

I found it refreshing to discover that the positive example and the loyalty of young students to their religious convictions had paved the way for the university's acceptance of my own. I have never felt that my conservative life-style and religious practice have been a hindrance to my career. Quite the contrary. Though I have never been one to wear my religion on my sleeve, I have found that in general it has earned me a measure of respect beyond whatever actual talents I may have for the profession. Regardless of whether they agree with your particular principles, other true professionals will likely respect your *loyalty* to those principles (as long as they are not dishonorable), and that goes just about as far.

By 1967, true to his original plan six years before, Murray was back working for the organization he loved—his church—cheerfully resuming his professional calling in life at about half the salary he had been making with Brakeley and the Ford Foundation at Guadalajara. His reentry into church employment had required some careful negotiation—not on salary, for that was standardized in church wage policy—but on the specific and unusual details of his desired job description.

When I left Mexico I had three solid and significant offers from other organizations, and enough contacts to generate even more. But I wanted to work for my church organization. My former superior at Brakeley, Lucien Escallier, said that he wanted me back. When I told him my desire, he said, "You're right. Your church needs you. Go back and work for them. But if it doesn't work out, I want to be the first to know."

Ironically, some of my Adventist friends were saying exactly the opposite: "Don't come back to the church; they won't appreciate you. You've got an excellent career going now. You have the experience, the credibility, and the contacts. This is your chance to make a real name for yourself and make some decent money." It made me a little sad to hear them say that.

Ever since I had left Loma Linda I'd had a pretty clear idea of my specific mission for the organization. By the time I finished my excursion with Brakeley and the Ford Foundation in Mexico, I was convinced that the only real way I could help was as a consultant. Church leaders at that time had a hard time grasping what I had in mind. They knew I was a fundraiser and so they thought I wanted a job raising money for one of our colleges or hospitals, and three or four institutions came forward with offers. But my idea was not so much that *I*, Milton Murray, raise money. Instead, I wanted to help these institutions set up ongoing programs that would become integral parts of their administrations.

So I stubbornly refused to be lured into an offer from any one institution. I believed that my expertise would best benefit the church at that time if I had a consulting relationship with many institutions, a few of which had already begun offices of development and public relations, but most of which had not.

My idea was a little like the classic juggler's act in which ten dinner plates are set spinning on the tops of ten freestanding sticks on a table. The goal is to get all ten going. The juggler starts the first plate spinning firmly on the first stick. It's easy. While momentum keeps the plate spinning, he starts the second and third plates. By the time he gets them going, the first plate is beginning to wobble badly, so he quickly intervenes and revives its spin. Then he starts the fourth plate. He repeats this pattern until at last all ten plates are spinning. That's what I wanted to do as a consultant for Adventist institutions—particularly those that had no program of their own, but also those that needed help with a program they had already started. If I had gotten attached to one institution, I would be spending my time keeping just one plate spinning very well. The other nine would be left sitting useless on the table. It would be a rather dull act, and it wouldn't have made the best use of my potential. Of course, the time might come when the institutions would become big enough to need a full-time, high-level professional fundraiser to keep each one going. That was the ultimate goal. But it was much too early for that. We needed modest beginnings at many institutions. That's what a consultant could do best.

Murray knew that church administrators wanted him back, but he also realized that his insistence on coming back as a consultant created a problem for them. What kind of employment relationship would this be? How would he be paid? Past experiences, from which church leaders may have innocently drawn the wrong conclusions, made it easy for them to be skeptical about consultants, believing that they generally swooped in to collect exorbitant fees for a few hours of marginally valuable advice. This wouldn't do in an organization that adhered to a firm "missionary" pay scale. If Murray wanted the life of a highly paid, jet-setting consultant, with church-backed entrée to institutions, would it be fair to consider him a church employee?

Murray, eagerly attempting to prove his good faith, made things easy. He simply asked for a regular church salary, just like any minister or teacher in the organization. The usual consulting fees paid by the client institutions would go, not to Murray, but to the central administrative organization to cover his salary and overhead expenses. And for Murray, that was the rub. He offered a service designed, in principle, to be revenue generating and self-supporting. This was unusual in his church's administrative structure. Typical of many corporate bureaucracies, the church sometimes staffed departments and services that were assumed to be necessary as much by the weight of tradition as by an actual understanding of their function. These services were not designed to generate revenue and could not be evaluated on that basis. In contrast, Murray had to convince the client institutions, through measurable results, that they needed him. If they didn't ask for his services, he would generate no revenue, and the business managers writing his paycheck would become nervous.

Murray's philosophy assumed nothing about the reception he would be given:

When you start something new, something you really believe in, you have to take risks. I could have chosen a safe, lucrative, professionally fulfilling job "outside," but my ultimate goal was to do something collectively for the hospitals and schools run by my church organization. Mine was a new idea. It wouldn't have been fair to expect that everyone would rush to endorse my concept. I had to prove its worth, and I couldn't expect to be given perks and job security while I was doing this.

I admire people who are willing to risk something for a new idea. When we began to get the page-a-day philanthropy calendar going, I worked with a woman at Workman Publishing named Margot Greenbaum Mustich. She is a great marketer. She's sharp, and she gave us a lot of help. Later she decided to leave Workman, and I was very disappointed. She wanted to become a columnist specializing in food. She went to work for a restaurant, starting out in the kitchen—cutting celery, cutting cabbage, making soup. I admired her for her bold decision, for the risks she was willing to take. I told the staff members in my office about her—that she had probably been making about $40,000 at Workman, and that she had left to work for less than half that amount in a restaurant kitchen. She wanted to know the business from the ground up. I told my workers, "If you want to succeed, you'll have to make that kind of choice someday. Don't look down on her for taking a 60 percent cut in salary. She's a smart woman. She knows what she's doing."

When I was negotiating the structure of my new job, my employers could see that I was willing to take risks, and they knew that I was absolutely loyal to the organization. To show my good faith, I told my employer, "All I ask is that you give me a year. You have no obligation. I'll take all the risk. If after those twelve months you decide that this idea is a dud, then give me thirty days' notice any time you want and I'll be gone. On the other hand, I'll promise you that I'll stay a minimum of three years. If my approach starts showing promise after a few months, you won't want to lose your investment by having me flit off like a butterfly to find an even better flower. I promise a minimum of three years. All you have to promise is one."

What did they have to lose with an offer like that?

I'm a firm believer in staying power. Three years may not sound like much and it is a lot less than my personal ideal of staying a minimum of five or six years. But I didn't want to scare them.

I know a man who's had a forty-year career. Every job he's had, with one six-year exception, saw him leave after eighteen months to two years. When he looks back on his career, how can he get any satisfaction out of it? What, of any significance, could he possibly have accomplished in a string of two-year jobs? He hasn't had a forty-year career; he's had a two-year career about seventeen times and has exhibited loyalty to nothing but himself. He's a butterfly, colorful and impressive, yes, but pushed about from place to place as much by the prevailing breeze as by any action of his wings, and always on the lookout for that easy drop of nectar. I think that's sad.

Contrast the butterfly to the honeybee, who systematically and patiently works the flowerbed, blossom by blossom. But then she loyally goes home, does a little dance to give directions, and invites others to return with her to collect the bounty. And, in a beneficial result entirely unknown to her, she pollinates the flowers.

At the far end of the honeybee continuum are people like my good friend Jim Frick at the University of Notre Dame. He devoted thirty-six years of his professional life to that institution, from 1950 until his retirement in 1986, with impressive results. I'm not necessarily claiming that one must go the extra mile as far as Jim took it, but it's not difficult to admire that kind of loyalty and dedication.

For Murray, the simplest measure of loyalty and dedication is productivity, and he sets a high standard. David Colwell, who worked for Murray for eight years, notes: "Milton expects a lot out of himself and his staff. You always have to put forth 100 percent and sometimes 150 percent. Many people don't want to do that. I'm a hard worker like Milton, so that's why I was able to work with him for so long. He can be very demanding and sometimes you might think unreasonable. I had no reason to think that, but I know that some people think they do."

Indeed. Murray is infamous in his organization for going through secretaries. During the 1980s, for example, Murray had seven different secretaries in seven years. Few were actually fired. They just decided to take other positions in the corporation. He recalls an incident from an earlier era when a new clerical worker, assigned to his department by the personnel office, showed up for her first day on the job, worked in the morning, went out for lunch, and never came back—not even to pick up her coat.

In his defense, he reminds his critics that in his career he has had several long-tenured secretaries, including Martha Sterner, who kept Murray's office humming perfectly for six years during a time when Murray averaged a day and a half in the office per month. "It takes a special kind of person to be able to do that, and that's the kind I work best with," he says. He also points out that in a recent downsizing at the Adventist World Headquarters office where he works, his office was one of the few left unscathed by substantial cutbacks in personnel. "I guess they were satisfied with our productivity," he says.

In a sense, Murray is a loyal misfit. Possessed of an independent, entrepreneurial spirit, developed both at Loma Linda and Brakeley, he has nevertheless devoted himself fervently to working within a bureaucratic world. His job, which he has created himself through the years, is defined only by the depth and breadth of his imagination. At the same time he has committed and confined himself to an organizational system of productivity that defines work less by the

limitless objects of the boss's imagination than by the limits
of time in the employee's thirty-eight-hour work week. Murray's best resolution to the inevitable tension between imagination and time is, simply, higher productivity, at a level that
is perhaps well beyond generally accepted standards. Some
people can handle it and some can't. And Murray, who is as
human as anyone, tends to measure or judge their commitment and loyalty to the cause by his own standard. "I have
difficulty adjusting to colleagues whose workmanship and
productivity reveal marginal commitment to the tasks at
hand," he says.

Murray's low-key and subtle style outside the office
wins him high praise from professional colleagues and donors,
and significant success in reaching his goals. His manner—
and manners—inside the office, however, carries a different
reputation. Murray can be brusque. Even his most ardent in-
house admirers acknowledge that he invests less time than
usual on pleasantries, particularly on the telephone, and that
he could afford to be more generous in his use of "please"
and "thank you."

A former secretary, who lasted as long as any, recalls a
steady barrage of "Where is it?" "How come you *don't*
know?" "Why isn't it done yet?" She says, "I left that job feeling that I wasn't equipped to do anything. I thought it was
all my fault. But I was encouraged when one of the senior
administrative secretaries in the corporation, overhearing an
exchange one day, told me: 'I would never allow him to talk
that way to me. You and the rest of his staff let him get away
with it. Everybody's afraid to stand up to him.' " Even his
defenders, who may claim that this particular secretary and
Murray were a mismatch from the start, recognize that seven
secretaries in seven years is not a good record.

For his part, Murray makes a distinction between the
issues of productivity and common office courtesy: "I'm a
fundraiser, a doer. Unfortunately for me, pioneering a program eventually leads to some managerial responsibilities.
I've never particularly enjoyed that or been very good at it. I
make plenty of mistakes. Some people think that I have some

real work to do on office manners, and maybe I do. But I won't excuse marginal performance in the warm glow of "good-buddyism," as important as that may be. I'm committed to this work and want to see it accomplished. I shouldn't have to convince people to be fully devoted to their tasks."

Whether this stark view is a Murray weakness, or ultimately a strength, as some see it, it is born out of an incontrovertible and absolute loyalty and commitment to two things: his profession and "the work."

His mother needn't have cried.

 10

A Grass-Roots Campaign in the Community: Making Philanthropy Meaningful to Main Street

> Remember, . . . there is no "ceiling" on philan-
> thropy. . . . Keep asking, keep raising sights, keep
> the "heat" on—because the money's there.
> —*Brakeley, 1980, p. 163*

When they told him that they would collect money in plastic buckets by stopping Sunday drivers on the two main intersections in and out of town, Milton Murray groaned.

This wasn't how it was supposed to be done. What would his colleagues from Brakeley think—or any New York professional, for that matter—when they heard about it? And they would hear about it. "Hey, remember Murray? A while back I heard he was doing a hospital campaign in some out-of-the-way town west of Newark. Well, I happened to drive through there last Sunday afternoon, and you're never going to believe what Murray's put those townfolks up to . . ."

To put it simply, Murray feared he would be laughed out of the profession.

Yet how could he squelch his volunteers' enthusiasm? He found their good-hearted, grass-roots sincerity a formidable counter to his sophisticated savoir faire. He couldn't expect them to think like experienced philanthropy professionals. And why should they worry about *his* professional reputation? They just wanted a hospital, and this was a way to get it. At the moment, Murray didn't have any better ideas.

The campaign for Hackettstown Community Hospital did, indeed, break some of the rules of fundraising practice. At the same time, according to Murray, who fondly reflects on the experience more than twenty years later, the campaign rigorously affirmed the theoretical foundation on which the profession rests. More important, he maintains, it proved his essential theory to be true, not just in the paneled gravity of corporate boardrooms or in the finely appointed upper-class sun rooms, but in the streets and storefronts and three-bedroom homes of middle America. Hackettstown intersected and integrated the diverse cultural perspectives inherent in the "philanthropy" of Mr. Fontaine, the foundation executive, and the "fundraising" of Mr. Fernandez, the corner florist.

Hackettstown, New Jersey, in 1968 was a city of twelve thousand in a farming region that was slowly changing to a light industrial economy. The monoliths of Manhattan loomed less than seventy miles away, yet still had remarkably little influence on day-to-day life. At 7:30 each weekday morning, six or eight of Hackettstown's twelve thousand residents huddled at the bus stop across from Plate's Jewelers to catch the Express line into the city.

The business district, wedged into four or five long blocks of Main Street, boasted mostly clapboard shop buildings, some brick storefronts with large plate-glass windows, a couple of banks and drugstores, a Strand theater, a sturdy brick United Methodist Church and an equally sturdy wood-frame, tall-steepled Presbyterian church. Except for the emphasis on wood instead of brick and stone, this could have passed for a slightly ragged twin of Bedford Falls, the fictional 1930s setting of the movie *It's a Wonderful Life.* Yet Hackettstown residents knew that change was coming. Interstate 80, under construction, crept west from Newark and would pass just a few miles north, at Allamuchy. The new highway promised to bring thousands of New Yorkers into the area, looking for a more rural environment, or so the Hackettstowners hoped. Of course, the new arrivals would contribute to the general economy. But equally important, in the minds of farmer, factory worker, and merchant alike, the projected influx of suburbanites would strengthen the argument for a hospital in town. The nearest one was seventeen miles away, in Newton.

Community leaders had been dreaming of a local hospital for more than twenty years. In the mid 1940s, some influential citizen or civic club first suggested the idea. Ten years of talking did little until 1955, when twenty-one townspeople boldly formed a corporation called Hackettstown Community Hospital, named themselves trustees, and chose Dan Allen, a sixty-year-old, well-to-do farmer as board president. Within a year, after organizing speeches in civic clubs and news stories and editorials in the Hackettstown *Star Gazette*, the trustees learned of a fifteen-acre lot available a half-mile out on the southeast side of town. This site could be a great place for a small modern hospital: plenty of room to breathe, to park, and someday to expand, in an area well clear of the clutter of the business and residential sections closer to the town center.

The corporation had little money and no credit rating, so the trustees paid the $22,500 purchase price out of their own pockets. Meanwhile, they pored over state licensing requirements and studied the New Jersey State Plan for Hospitals. They also traveled around the state visiting hospitals similar to the one they had in mind. Repeatedly, officials told them that Hackettstown ranked low on the state's priority list, and that it couldn't support even the most modest of hospitals. Meanwhile, the state kept raising its definition of "modest." Originally, trustees envisioned a twenty-five-bed facility, the minimum allowed by state guidelines. About the time such a hospital began to seem feasible, the state raised the minimum to fifty beds, then one hundred. An architect advised them of the futility of their dreams. Construction estimates seemed unreasonably high and lending institutions said that the paper hospital corporation didn't have a strong enough financial base on which to borrow money.

Ten years slipped by in a relentless cycle of hope and despair, but mostly despair. Doggedly, Dan Allen and the other trustees kept the momentum of the property purchase going by holding regular monthly board meetings, even when the agenda presented nothing to discuss. They engineered articles in the *Star Gazette* and made more speeches in civic clubs.

In 1967, more than twenty years after the hospital first became a dream, a chance conversation took place in a Main Street banker's office that markedly influenced the history of Hackettstown. Ironically, it occurred in the setting of another philanthropic enterprise. Murray has told the story a hundred times since, though he was not a party to the occasion.

For most of this century, Seventh-day Adventists have run a program each fall to solicit funds from the general public in order to support their worldwide health, welfare, and disaster-relief programs. They call it Harvest Ingathering. Members ring doorbells in neighborhoods near their churches, briefly explain the program, and ask for donations. The pastor usually makes the calls on local businesses, sometimes in the company of a businessperson from the congregation. In 1968, Harvest Ingathering brought in nearly seven million dollars, so it was an important church program.

One day two Adventist ministers from a nearby town called on Henry Roerich, a Hackettstown farmer and chairman of one of the two banks in town. They sat in Roerich's office, from which they could look out onto the Main Street sidewalk through large plate glass windows. As Roerich and the two ministers talked about Harvest Ingathering, Roerich suddenly said, "Look, you people run hospitals all over the world. We've been trying to get one for twenty years. Why don't you help us get one in Hackettstown?"

A moment later Frank DeLello, one of the hospital trustees, walked by on the sidewalk. Roerich knocked on the window and motioned him to come into the office. When DeLello entered, Roerich said, "Frank, these men are Adventist ministers. Adventists run hospitals all around the world. I think the hospital trustees should get together with these people and see if it's possible to figure out a way to get us a hospital." DeLello said he'd check it out.

Six weeks later Roerich saw Dan Allen on the street. Allen, still president of the hospital trustees, was also a member of the board of the other bank in town and had known Roerich well for about forty years. Roerich said, "Dan, whatever came of the idea I suggested to DeLello about having Adventists help us with the hospital?" Allen said, "Well, we discussed it and decided not to do it." To which Roerich replied, "Now Dan, how did you discuss it? If you just chatted for a few minutes around the table, that won't do. I'm talking about really checking this organization out in depth. Talk to some of their people. Get some of their specialists up here. If you do this and decide not to work with them, I'll accept it."

Before long, the committee began talking with officials of the church's Columbia Union Conference, the administrative office that supervised operations in a seven-state Mid-Atlantic region, including the newly opened Kettering Medical Center in Dayton, Ohio. Specialists from Kettering and another church-run hospital in Maryland made a quick visit to Hackettstown in the fall of 1967 and told church leaders that a hospital in Hackettstown had potential. Their report prompted officials to send Murray, who had recently signed on as resident consultant for the Columbia Union Conference, to the small New Jersey town to take a closer look.

I went up there with Oliver Jacques, the PR man from Hadley Memorial Hospital, to conduct a more formal feasibility study. Church officials introduced us to the members of the hospital committee at a luncheon at the Musconetcong Country Club. I made a little presentation and told them that Jacques and I would visit people around town in the next four or five days to conduct short interviews.

As the meeting broke up, Dan Allen came over to me and said, "Come see me the first chance you get." I said I would. But I didn't want to talk to him first, because he was the chairman. I needed to have more of a feel for the circumstances before I talked with him. He represented the leadership. He *was* the leadership. If I, in my humble staff responsibility, was supposed to lead the leaders, I needed more information before tipping my hand in any way.

For the next two or three days, Oliver and I became a spectacle on the streets of Hackettstown. It was a small place, and word spread rapidly up and down Main Street that there were fundraisers in town. They didn't know exactly what we were doing but it was clear that we were a popular topic for barbershop speculation. We visited some of the small merchants and asked questions about their businesses and those of others in the town. We talked informally about the hospital and tried to gauge their level of emotional and financial commitment to the idea.

Toward the end of the first day, two women, in separate incidents, stopped me on the street. Each one asked if I was there to help raise money for the hospital and told me I ought to go see Mr. Allen. "He's got a lot of money," they said. "Oh really? How much do you think he'd give?" Both of them said that he ought to give $5,000. I thanked them for their help.

I went to see Dan Allen the next day. He was about seventy-eight years old, a stocky man about five feet eight inches tall. Whenever he was away from home, he always wore a hat, and this was after the age of hats. We sat on his sun porch and he began to talk.

I listened carefully because he was the leader and because I could tell that I really was going to like him. He said, "Let me tell you something. I've lived here all my life except for six months when I worked in New York. Hackettstown has been good to me. But you know, I lost my wife eight years ago and I've sometimes wondered whether they could have saved her if we'd had a hospital close by."

I didn't inquire into the particulars because I didn't want to interrupt his flow of thought. He continued, "I've always wanted a hospital. Ever since she died, I've been committed to getting one for this town. I've thought about this a lot. And I want to give $50,000. I can't pay it all right now, but I have ways of getting it. I can pay within the next two or three years. You can put this information to work for you as you see fit."

Then he paused, and I could tell that something important was coming. He said, "And there's something else I want to tell you. But it's got to be very confidential." I replied, "Mr. Allen, I live on secrets." He then said, "I've put the hospital in my will. The hospital will get virtually all of my estate."

I said nothing, and he let that hang in the air for a moment. And then he added, "I suppose I ought to tell you how much that amounts to. Well, I don't know, but here are a few figures. Do you have a piece of paper? Start writing."

For the next few minutes he stared off over the valley, seeing items in his mind as though he were reading them from a ledger on the opposite hill. He'd call out an item, pause for a moment, and give a dollar figure. Bank stocks, savings accounts, parcels of real estate in and around Hackettstown, and some elsewhere in New Jersey.

Meanwhile I scribbled away with my pencil, trying to keep up with him. When he finished his recitation, I added up the figures. The total came to

$523,000. Remember that this was in 1968, before the great inflation of the 1970s. Mr. Allen was not talking about a small amount of money.

He continued: "Now this matter can't be shared with anybody. I guess you can tell your boss back at your headquarters, but that's about it."

I left Mr. Allen's home on Quarry Hill feeling very good about the prospects of the hospital. Although his $50,000 contribution was all we could make public, my superiors could have confidence that the Hackettstown community could do its part—especially if there were more people in town who had the values and the vision, if not the money, of Dan Allen. During the next two years, I chatted with him almost every week on that sun porch and I quickly came to respect and love this businesslike but altruistic man, a true pillar of small-town America.

The next day I went to see Fred Cook, the owner of a company that made the dyes for the colors used in the insulation on telephone wires. Cook's company was one of the largest operations in town, and Cook may have been the wealthiest man on the hospital board. His personal worth was probably several times that of Allen.

Mr. Cook got to the point quickly because he knew that I was there about the hospital. He said, "Murray, I'll tell you right up front that I have no intention of buying this town a hospital." It seemed to me that this was his way of saying that he felt the only reason he'd been put on the board was because everyone was hoping he'd underwrite the entire hospital.

So I said, "Mr. Cook, I don't blame you a bit. I wouldn't do that either, if I were you. And I'm not here to ask for money. I'm here to get a feel for the community and see if this idea is even feasible. I'll know in a few more days. But I can tell you one thing. Mr. Allen just told me yesterday that he is going to give a substantial gift. He's talking about

$50,000. I'm not sure that's to be commonly known yet, but it's a fact."

Cook smiled, threw himself back in his chair, and said, "That's interesting. If it's true, then you can also count on this company making a . . . substantial gift."

Just moments before, I had intentionally—but in an offhand manner—defined "substantial gift." Without having to be specific with Mr. Cook, I left his office knowing that I could count on at least $50,000.

Two days later, Mr. Cook had a heart attack. The ambulance took him the seventeen miles over bumpy roads to the nearest hospital. I think he realized that it would have been convenient to have a hospital a little closer to home. His company ended up giving $80,000.

After more conversations around town, Murray was ready to make an initial report to the hospital board. No record or specific recollections exist of Murray's informal oral report. His brief written report was typical of his style. Murray does not like to be blunt. His first sentence put reality in the gentlest of terms: "It must be recognized that potential participating agencies and organizations would become involved more readily if the Hackettstown community and adjacent areas were to demonstrate interest and commitment for at least 25 percent of the total cost."

However he wrote it, Murray's bottom line was clear: You folks in Hackettstown have to deliver, or there's no help from my organization, and probably no hospital. Happily, Murray's next sentence promised good news. His study concluded that the people of Hackettstown could, "with proper leadership," obtain up to $750,000 and with extra effort could even raise $900,000, about 23 percent of the projected $4 million cost. This, Murray indicated, was close enough to satisfy his organization's interest in investing in the enterprise.

How did he arrive at the $900,000 figure (which did not include Allen's promised bequest)?

You give yourself a margin, say a prayer, and make a pronouncement. There is only so much research you can do for an initial feasibility study. To get the project going, you have to make some guesses. And like those of any other philanthropy professional, mine were educated guesses, based on my previous experience. But Hackettstown was a different world from that of my Brakeley days in Phoenix or my time with the Ford Foundation in Guadalajara. This was Small Town U.S.A. With the exception of a few people like Allen and Cook, we were looking at plain folks trying to raise that amount of money from their own pockets, the shops on Main Street, and a few local companies.

Murray wasn't surprised, however, when the trustees became enthusiastic and started talking about raising the goal to a million dollars. When they asked him if this was possible, Murray said, "Sure, you can do anything if you give yourself enough time. Is this what you want to do?" They answered, "Yes!"

I thought it wouldn't do any great harm if they talked about a million dollars, but I also knew that I would have to bring them back to earth by explaining the implications of their enthusiasm. In the lively discussion that followed, someone said that I should plan to see the M&M/MARS plant, which was nearby. I said, "Yes, someone has to see them one of these days, but there's something we have to do before that."

They asked, "What's that? What's the next step?" I said, "You, the trustees, have to put up the first money yourselves." They agreed and asked how much they should give. "Well," I said, "the rule of thumb in a campaign like this is that the trustees come up with 40 percent."

That hit them pretty hard.

"That's $400,000! Murray, we're just shop owners." "I know," I said. "That's why it intrigued

me that you wanted to go up to a million. I'm willing
to settle for $750,000.''

The trustees, by now forming clear ideas of the kind of
hospital they wanted, remained committed to the million-
dollar goal. Murray, equally stubborn, maintained his insistence on their 40 percent, a figure they knew was beyond
their reach. However amicable their relationship, Murray and
the trustees were deadlocked.

We sweated over this for a couple of meetings. It
became clear to me that if I held them to the 40 percent, there would never be a hospital. This wasn't a
board for one of the Big Five symphonies, or a Big
Ten university, that can draw its members from high
society all over the country. This was a small-town
hospital, whose board members all lived within ten
miles of their empty lot. The formula had to be
adjusted to fit the circumstances. So I finally said,
"Let's try 25 percent. I won't come down any farther."
     They agreed to the 25 percent, but it was clear
that it would still be a struggle for them, even with
Allen's $50,000 accounting for more than a fifth of
their goal right at the start.
     I did some rationalizing and decided that they
should get credit for the land they had purchased
twelve years earlier. The land was worth $75,000, so we
counted that toward their goal. I fudged things a little
because the land price hadn't been counted in the overall million-dollar community goal. Theoretically, add-
ing in the land value should have made the community goal $1.075 million, which would have raised
the trustees' portion to $268,750. I chose to let it go.
     Within a few weeks they reached $238,000,
which came in in small amounts. Then the contributions stopped. I felt that I couldn't let them off. I had
made two major concessions already, on their percent-

age and by giving them credit for the land. They *had* to come through with a solid $250,000.

During this time, Murray consulted for several other institutions around the country and still did work sponsored by the Ford Foundation in Latin America. Yet he spent more time in Hackettstown than anywhere else, even though his main office and his family were based in Dayton, Ohio. Hackettstown grew on him.

I had never really had a hometown. I had spent my formative years—the time when roots are formed—as part of a mission family in South America, and we moved a lot. Then I lived in college dormitories or army barracks in Alaska and in veterans' housing until I was in my mid twenties and began my professional life. I had very few roots anywhere. I liked Hackettstown and adopted it as my place in the world. I loved the people, and I always liked listening to their stories and hearing about their squabbles.

When I was in town I stayed at a place called the Clarendon Hotel. It was an old building in the middle of a downtown block and typified the inexorable but gentle decline of the hotel in small-town America. The place had seen better days. It *must* have. The charge was about eight dollars per night. During my time there, the Clarendon slowly began to drift out of business. The number of night workers grew smaller. The restaurant closed. By the end of my sojourn in Hackettstown it was still a hotel, but it was having a tough time. Often I arrived in town late at night after the reception desk closed. I'd come into the hotel by a service door in the back and walk through the kitchen and out to the dark reception desk. I'd feel around in the cabinets until I found a room key, and I'd let myself in. The next morning I'd tell the desk clerk I'd stayed there, and I'd pay for my room. The time came when there wouldn't be a clerk on duty when I left in the morning, so I'd just leave a check in an envelope on the desk. That's the kind of great little place Hackettstown was.

The next time I met with the trustees, I told them, "We've got to get moving if we're going to get this job done. I'm going back to Dayton, and when I come back next week, you've got to have that $250,000."

I came back the next week and they were still stuck at $238,000. They had been counting on the physicians to help them. That was another concession I had made. I allowed them to include the physicians with the trustees, which really wasn't correct practice. The $250,000, already a low figure, really should have come from the bona fide leadership—those who had signed their names on the dotted line. The physicians were not part of that group, but the trustees had asked if they could be included to help share the "leadership" role in giving. Although the trustees had high hopes for the help they would get from the physicians, my experience with physicians in other hospital campaigns had suggested something different. The only reason I allowed the physicians to be counted with the trustees was that I didn't think it would make much difference in the total.

And I was right. At the risk of stereotyping, let me explain my judgment. As a general rule, physicians are idealists who view themselves as already being immersed in working for the direct welfare of humanity. Rightly or wrongly, they often object to being expected to do more by giving their money. Many of them believe that monetary philanthropy should be the duty of those who are engaged in less humanitarian professions. Even if my analysis is incorrect or simplistic, it has been borne out by my experience, including that of Hackettstown. The trustees were disappointed and I was not surprised.

When I returned from Dayton, nothing had happened. By this time I was becoming a little impatient. I took care of some immediate business and sent word that I was leaving for good. This wasn't a ploy. I couldn't stay around forever relying on their hopes and wishes. It sounds a little petty for the success of the entire operation, including the major backing of my organization, to come down to $12,000. But I had to insist on some basics. At the same time, this was not an easy thing to do. These were real people, with real hopes and real dreams and real problems. This wasn't some large, impersonal, big-city campaign where supporters hedge their bets and don't become too emotionally committed. There was total emotional commitment here. Many of these people had already invested hundreds or thousands of hours in the hospital. And what did they have to show for it? An empty lot. It was tough to look them in the eye and say,"I'm leaving."

I told Dan Allen, "Call up the other members of your committee and tell them that unless they come up with another $12,000, we're through—and I'm leaving." Allen asked me to reconsider, and I answered, "I'll tell you what I will do. If you call a meeting for six o'clock tonight, and you can get the $250,000 before your regular board meeting at eight o'clock, I'll hang around and see what happens."

He urged me to attend the six o'clock meeting. I reluctantly agreed but made it clear that I would have nothing to say. They were the leaders and were going to have to show it. Allen opened the meeting by saying, "Mr. Murray has told me that he's leaving town unless we have our $250,000 by eight o'clock. We're $12,000 short. I am going to put in another $3,000."

In the same way in which his original pledge had influenced Mr. Cook a few weeks earlier, it influenced the others around the table at this dramatic moment. After a long pause, someone else spoke up: "Well, I can add another thousand." Then another: "I can manage fifteen hundred."

I sat quietly at the side, listening and writing down sums on a piece of paper. It took nearly the full two hours, but they finally had reached the $12,000 and their $250,000 goal.

The board meeting followed at eight o'clock. Everyone was feeling good. Mr. Allen told them briefly, "We are now on track with the necessary amount from the trustees, and Mr. Murray is pleased." And indeed I was. It was a great day. They had passed a major milestone in the campaign and they were really *leading*. Hackettstown would have a hospital. Somebody asked, "So what's the next step?" I said, "We've got to start working on the corporations."

Allen and Murray had originally planned that Fred Cook would lead the campaign for the corporations, but he was still recovering from his heart attack. In his stead the trustees chose John Henderson, the plant manager at Cook's company, to lead this aspect of the campaign. Henderson soon called a meeting of representatives from the five major companies in the area. He told them that the campaign needed $800,000 from the corporations and that they would soon receive proposals. Murray delivered some of the proposals that same day.

We used straightforward, standard formulas for campaigns for new hospitals. We established goals for the corporations based on the number of employees they had, what percentage lived in the area to be serviced by the hospital, and so forth.

At Henderson's first meeting, we gave the M&M/MARS plant in town a proposal for $400,000. When the M&M/MARS representative saw it, he nearly fainted. But he also knew that the company had to give. It was the biggest company in town at the time. If there was going to be corporate leadership in this campaign, it had to start here.

A few days later, I met with the M&M/MARS officer. He didn't think our request for $400,000 made much sense, and he produced some data showing that only two-thirds of his employees lived in the hospital service area. So we made some adjustments and renegotiated the figure to $250,000. He was still gloomy about selling the idea to his company leadership.

Apparently the gloom had some foundation in prevailing views at M&M/MARS headquarters. Word came back that the company was not in a position to make a contribution. Murray recalls:

I can still see the faces around the room during the board meeting when we announced the M&M/MARS plant decision. I told the board that we wouldn't have much of a program if M&M/MARS wasn't going to come through. It was a dark moment. Some of the women cried, and some of men probably wanted to.

We realized later that we were pressing M&M/MARS too hard. They needed a little more time to make their decision, and until they had that time, they simply chose to say no. They knew very little about the Adventist hospital system. The community intended to turn ownership and control of the new hospital over to this organization. But could the town really be sure that these outsiders really knew what they were doing and could be trusted? Obviously, the hospital trustees and other community leaders were satisfied. But, quite appropriately, M&M/MARS plant officers wanted some verification of their own. They didn't want to waste their money on a bad idea.

While we were crying over M&M/MARS's rejection notice, the company quietly flew some representatives out to Loma Linda University Medical Center to look around. When they returned, the plant manager at the local plant called me in and promised to come through with a one-for-two matching program up to $250,000. I would have been happier with a straight grant, but it was an excellent start. M&M/ MARS agreed to pay on cash only—not pledges. At the end of six months, we had $14,000 in hand from the corporations. I took a photostat of our record sheet over to the financial officer, and he authorized a check for $7,000. This became a ritual every six months.

As the months went on, the campaign progressed. The corporations exceeded their own expectations. By September 1968, the trustees, encouraged by the progress among the corporations, publicly announced a community campaign of $1.6 million, more than half again the amount they had haggled over just a few months before. At the same time, the Seventh-day Adventist Church promised $750,000 as its share beyond the community effort. The balance of funding was to come from an anticipated grant of $1 million available through the federal government's Hill-Burton program, and from commercial financing.

It looked hopeful for the hospital campaign until May 1969, when the Hill-Burton grant was sliced in half. The blow increased the community burden by $500,000. In June 1970, eager leaders were again dismayed when construction bids came in much higher than anticipated. Already pressed to the limit, the community could hardly be expected to take on the full additional difference of $600,000. Adventist church members throughout New Jersey agreed to come up with $350,000, in addition to the basic grant from the parent church organization, which had already been raised by $100,000 to $850,000.

The financial hurdles, daunting enough at the start, had become more forbidding. Instead of the $4 million hospital of 1967, residents of Hackettstown and its environs were now trying to build a $7.2 million facility. In three years' time, their own out-of-pocket share had increased nearly 300 percent, from $900,000 to $2.7 million.

While Murray and the campaign leaders were working on the corporations, another campaign was pressing ahead among the residents themselves. Murray says, "Oliver Jacques, my colleague from Hadley Memorial Hospital, came in to organize a door-to-door campaign. He attended breakfasts and brunches, made presentations, and organized women's groups. We didn't ask for $5 or $10. We asked for $100 and $200. And, incredibly, people came through. They really believed in the hospital. We raised hundreds of thousands of dollars in that way."

In fact, the Hackettstown campaign depended heavily on small gifts. As Murray noted in a summary report written in 1972 near the end of the campaign, the campaign did not follow the typical formula then operative in prevailing fundraising theory: 50 percent from the ten largest donors; 35 percent from the next hundred donors; and 15 percent from all others. At the end of the first year, the first ten donors accounted for 46 percent of the receipts or pledges, the next hundred donors represented 26 percent, and the remaining small donors contributed 28 percent. By the end of the campaign three years later, these figures were even more dramatic. The top ten donors brought in only 35 percent, the next hundred represented 23.7 percent, and the thousands of small donations made up more than 41 percent.

Murray explained this by noting that as the campaign progressed, more and more money was required to meet the goal. The large donors had already reached their limit. As the demand increased, small gifts remained the only unexhausted source of funding.

The smallest gifts of all came from the portion of the campaign that worried Murray the most and provoked his only real altercation with the board. Early in the get-acquainted stage, Murray had asked the trustees how the community intended to pay for the costs of the campaign. He reminded them that it costs money to raise money, and he explained that although his salary would be covered by his organization, the campaign needed an office with equipment and secretarial help, heat, lights, and a telephone. Where would the money come from?

They hadn't thought about that. And they insisted that not one cent of their contributions would pay for the fundraising expense. They quite naturally wanted it all to go into their hospital. I explained that capital campaigns usually built administrative costs into the overall goal, but they insisted that they didn't want to do that.

Then someone suggested that they simply ask for money on the street corners from passersby. I was horrified. I couldn't let them do that. That was begging. Furthermore, I believed that it would undercut serious giving from the local citizenry. We had quite a lively discussion about that, and I wasn't going to give in. But neither were they. They agreed to limit the collection to weekend motorists passing through town during the summer months. From their perspective, it was a good strategy. Anyone driving between New York and the Poconos had to go right through Hacketts-town, so there were plenty of potential "donors." I consented to their scheme, but under loud protest.

Bill Rossi coordinated this part of the campaign. Everybody knew Bill and liked him. He ran a milk wholesale business and owned the local Dairy Queen. He also had been influential in the community effort to persuade M&M/MARS to locate a plant in town. Each weekend between May 1 and Labor Day he organized different community groups, civic clubs, and churches to staff the Bucket Brigade, or Coin Toss, as it became more popularly known. Armed with plastic buckets and placards proclaiming "Help Our Hospital," and sometimes dramatically dressed up in bandages and hobbling on crutches, ten to twelve people policed each of the two key intersections on Route 46 in and out of town. I think that Rossi was out there himself about two-thirds of the time. The volunteers had amazing dedication. It was *their* project, *their* way of doing things. By the end of the first summer, they had collected more than

$25,000, and I grudgingly admitted that they may have had a good idea. But I still cringed at the damage this could do to the reputation of professional fundraising.

The Hackettstown *Star Gazette* gave the Coin Toss a high profile, reporting weekly totals and helping in other ways to keep spirits up and community groups willing to participate. Tourists driving back and forth to the Poconos weren't always pleased with the resulting traffic jam and sometimes complained. Some even claimed that the state was deliberately holding up completion of Interstate 80 until the hospital campaign was over. (Ironically, Interstate 80 opened for general use within days after the hospital's official opening.)

After three more summers, the Coin Toss had netted more than $100,000, all in pocket change and dollar bills. One trucker from the Midwest passed through Hackettstown every Friday on a run to New York. Each time, he stopped his semi in the road and faithfully wrote out a five-dollar check. One of the largest contributions in that huge amount of money was a twenty-dollar bill from another trucker who passed through regularly. He thought that a town with so many steep hills and narrow roads needed a good hospital nearby. The Coin Toss turned into a grass-roots triumph and more than covered the remarkably low overhead costs of the campaign—about 3 percent. I decided that you can't argue with success.

The Coin Toss immediately began paying expenses at the campaign office, which leaders rented on the first floor of a building on Main Street owned by a jeweler with a shop next door. The campaign office had a total work area about thirty feet wide and seventy feet deep. Halfway back, a flimsy partition with a door created a separate meeting room. The two or three office workers sat at old wooden desks. Residents and local businesses donated old typewriters, other used office equipment, paper and supplies to help keep down expenses.

The office had no mimeograph machine and used the copy equipment at the M&M/MARS plant.

As the campaign progressed, the office space became crammed with cubicles and desks, not for additional fundraising staff, but for the administrative personnel of the new hospital itself, including the president, a vice president for finance, a director and assistant director of nurses, a lab director, and the requisite support staff.

Hospital president Charley Eldridge took up residence in the campaign office about two years into the campaign. Geneva Bulford, who worked for four years recording campaign receipts, recalls that he began to establish a professional image for the as-yet-nonexistent hospital as well as he could within the limitations of the office space.

He also learned to appreciate the interesting working style of his campaign colleagues, including Adeline Geisler— a woman in her sixties and a hospital trustee who volunteered nearly full-time for the campaign. Geneva Bulford recalls:

Adeline mothered us in the office and took responsibility for handling the money. We kept the office open each day much later than the banks, and we usually had a large amount of money that couldn't be deposited until the following morning. We had no safe in the office, so it wasn't a good idea to leave the money in the office overnight. Adeline took it upon herself to safeguard the money. She had heard somewhere that robbers would never suspect that anyone was carrying a large amount of money in a brown paper bag. Each evening she'd stuff the day's cash and checks—sometimes several thousand dollars—into a paper bag, lock herself in her car, and head toward her home several miles out of town. Adeline wasn't a confident driver under the best of circumstances, and when she carried all this money she preferred to drive right down the middle of the road to foil would-be robbers. The next morning she headed back into town in the same fashion to make the bank deposit and come to work.

By early 1972, the protracted campaign wore thin. The community's contribution remained $300,000 short of its finally adjusted goal of $2.7 million, with very little prospect of finding more sources of money. Murray knew that it was time to turn to foundations, believing that they could not help but be favorably impressed by the willing spirit, hard work, and remarkable achievement of the citizens of Hackettstown. More than fifty foundations were contacted with proposals or personal queries. Dozens of polite refusals came back in the next few weeks, but spirits were not dampened. Hackettstown rode high on the news that one of the first foundations to respond—Kresge—promised a $100,000 matching grant if the remaining $200,000 could be raised by December 15, 1972. The community met the deadline.

In an ironic twist of circumstance that delighted everyone and evoked a sheepish blush from Murray, campaign leaders learned that a Kresge Foundation official had been caught one Sunday in the traffic jam of the Hackettstown Coin Toss. What his view happened to be at that moment is not known, but months later, when the Hackettstown proposal came to his attention, he remembered the incident, and Hackettstown got the grant.

"Needless to say," Murray observes philosophically, "I've had to eat a lot of humble pie."

Perhaps, but not as much as some philanthropy professionals might have had to swallow, Murray's admirers claim. Murray has great respect for the average citizen—the farmer, the mechanic, the cashier. Although his profession requires him to mix easily with corporate executives and the affluent in high society, his humble heritage as the son of missionary parents and his own lower-middle-class station keeps him current with common humanity.

"When Milton came to Hackettstown, people believed him," says Geneva Bulford. "Other fundraisers had come through to investigate the hospital plans, and they left a bad impression. But right from the start, people knew they could trust Milton. He was dead earnest and honest, and there was nothing slick about him. The people of Hackettstown loved him for it. He was one of them."

Groundbreaking ceremonies for the hospital had been held in August 1970. Amid the excitement, there was a note of sadness. Dan Allen was missing. About six weeks before the planned festivities, Murray visited with Allen, who then was more than eighty years old. Murray later wrote of that visit:

> For more than two years I had frequented the house on Quarry Hill. The sun porch had been silent witness to the late-afternoon chats I had once a week with Dan Allen. As a prominent and lifelong resident of Hackettstown, Allen had achieved the status of elder statesman among the community's leaders. His physical vigor and mental acuity belied his eighty years. . . .
>
> But recently Allen had been ill and was under a physician's care. His health was not what it had been. I had dropped by Quarry Hill to greet him and tell him we looked forward to his presence at the groundbreaking ceremonies, hoping against hope that he would be able to attend. As I recall that conversation, we both seemed to have a premonition that it would be our last.
>
> I reassured him that his leadership and generosity had in great measure made the hospital project a reality. He, in turn, insisted that the Seventh-day Adventist Church, through its know-how and expertise, had made it possible. Without minimizing the contribution of the church to the establishment of the hospital, I reassured him: "Mr. Allen, the church has been happy to cooperate with this community and to invest its know-how and staff. However, you played the early role. You gave substantially. You led us all to this point. Your leadership was essential to its success."
>
> I had already gotten up from my chair and was turning to go when Allen motioned me to delay my

departure. He looked out over the valley—scenery we had both so often enjoyed—and in a low voice and reverent tone said, "Well, that may or may not be so. But what I do know is that my having been involved in the hospital has made me a better Christian."

Those were the last words I heard from Allen's lips.

Three years later, Hackettstown Community Hospital stood ready to be dedicated and officially opened. According to the agreement, the hospital board, which had existed since 1955, signed over ownership and operation to the Adventist Church. It had been a long struggle, a sweat-and-tears struggle of ordinary people who made their dream come true in the ordinary way. Murray could take his own share of pride in their monumental accomplishment. Like any resourceful professional, he had adjusted his methods to local circumstances. He also learned that raising money by the bucket isn't such a bad idea after all.

Charley Eldridge, the hospital administrator, planned the opening events and anticipated a crowd of about a thousand people. Five thousand Hackettstown residents showed up. It was their day.

Conclusion:
The Fundraiser's
Contribution
to Philanthropy

No person has ever been honored for what he
received. Honor has been the reward for what he
gave.
> —*Calvin Coolidge,*
> *as quoted in Forbes, Inc.,*
> *1976, p. 397*

What's the difference between a great fundraiser and a great
philanthropist?

The question sounds like the perfect setup for a punch
line destined to appear in a future edition of *Accent on
Humor,* Milton Murray's book about the lighter side of
philanthropy.

But here the question is asked seriously. If pressed, Murray will maintain that there is very little difference—except
wealth. Both the genuine philanthropic fundraiser and the
genuine philanthropist are preoccupied with making the
world a better place. It is simply that one specializes in the
ways and the other in the means. They share the same spirit,
which is the essential element.

196

This is why Murray and some of his colleagues have been arguing persistently, if unsuccessfully, for years against the term *fundraising* to describe their profession. They advocate its replacement with forms—however awkward—of the word *philanthropy*. Murray claims that for a time, some were even advocating seriously the use of the term "philanthropoid" to describe practitioners. Close readers of this book will note that the term *fundraiser* has rarely been left without the qualifying adjective *philanthropic*.

Thus, the lines between asker and giver become increasingly indistinct, as Murray and others believe they should. Fundraising possibilities transform themselves into "philanthropic possibilities" to someone who, in Murray's romantic vision, is not a fundraiser at all but a "laborer in the vineyards of philanthropy," a concept he borrowed and adapted from Harold Seymour. Murray likes the phrase, uses it often, and doubtless is attracted to it by its not-so-subtle biblical allusion.

Murray and others believe, perhaps rightly, that the term *fundraiser* carries with it the faint aura of pass-the-hat hucksterism. For many, fundraising now connotes the extraction of money from an unwilling subject. In the purest sense, Murray argues, donors give voluntarily and without insistence on the part of another person. He believes, however, that perhaps because of some shaky professionalism in the past, popular usage has practically transformed the term into a pejorative. Thus, Murray fears, fundraisers rank in public esteem somewhere in the company of used car salespeople, politicians, and TV evangelists. He recalls an incident that demonstrates this attitude.

> Twenty-five years ago I was doing some consulting work for a two-year college that had been in operation about three years. A new academic dean came on board and I told him that we really should start an alumni annual fund. After all, there had been a few years of graduates, and it was time for us to begin organizing ourselves to work with them on a consistent basis. So I asked the dean for a list of graduates.

A few days later, the dean came into my office, dropped some paper on my desk, and said, "Here's the list you wanted. I'm eager to see how you con them out of money."

I couldn't let this opportunity pass. It was a teachable moment. I told him, "My friend, if that's your point of view, I'm not going to be able to do anything for you. Your alumni should be giving out of loyalty and appreciation for what this institution has done for them. If you think you have to 'con them out of money,' that means you don't deserve it, and if you don't deserve it, then I can't help you."

Granted, many things can change in twenty-five years. Societal attitudes about a vocation can, over time, be significantly enhanced. But the battle never ends. Once, while this book was being written, Murray attended a meeting of church officials where he was introduced by an influential physician as "the chief person here at headquarters who goes around the country conning people into giving money."

"This time, I let it go," Murray says. "It wasn't the time to embarrass him in front of his peers, and he probably thought he was being funny." But it is clear that for Murray, and doubtless for hundreds of other professionals, the jokes wear thin after twenty or thirty years.

The struggle for more positive professional nomenclature has not been easy. The primary professional society for practitioners like Murray is the National Society of Fund-Raising Executives. Until the profession itself, as represented by its most significant organization, takes up the cause, little is likely to happen. But Murray and others keep chipping away. And they are seeing some hopeful signs. The National Association for Hospital Development recently changed its name to the Association for Healthcare Philanthropy. And Murray has rejoiced at the recent suggestions he has heard for changing NSFRE to the Council for the Advancement of Philanthropy.

"For all my talk on this subject, I'm embarrassed that I

didn't think of that sooner myself. I think that name has great potential, and I would heartily endorse it."

For all Murray's talk on the subject of nomenclature, he would be one of the first to claim that names or titles are not the things that really earn professional respect. Doing the work and doing it well will win the day more easily than having the right title or association name. Form follows function, and style follows substance.

Some of Murray's substance has been identified in the qualities, assets, characteristics, and approaches to life and work detailed in this book. His energy, efficiency, and productivity are legend among his office and professional colleagues, many of them decades younger. His family heritage and life experience as a young adult sparked in him an evolving professional calling that might be found in the lives of thousands today if only it could be brought to their attention.

Murray's old-fashioned "American ingenuity" has taught him that there is always some way to solve a problem. Creativity is not so much an inherent quality as an acquired trait. You have to work at it, he claims. And he does.

Murray finds that leadership often builds on creativity, as the creative or innovative person recommends or blazes the path for others to follow. Thus, leadership for Murray is as much a natural outgrowth or result of other characteristics as it is a specific activity in itself. It just happens, and yet it is the obligation of any professional to make sure that it happens.

Related to the obligation of leadership is Murray's passion for those who will follow after. He finds ways to involve and mentor young people in the work of philanthropy and then admires the sometimes awesome results of their enthusiasm.

Youth, however, without the perspective that age can bring, often undervalues the dogged persistence that has been a hallmark of some of Murray's greatest successes and unrealized dreams. He stubbornly refuses to give in, even in the face of relentless disappointment, for he has too often eventually seen the rewards.

Those rewards come more often to those who are willing to let others have most of the credit. Murray is such a man. Anonymity on the part of the philanthropic fundraiser keeps the focus on the CEOs, volunteers, and donors who must be perceived as the leaders in philanthropic enterprise. Thus, this vocation finds its most admired practitioners accomplishing more as stage managers than as stars.

Loyalty and commitment to the profession and even to an organization is more necessary in philanthropy than in many other careers. Success often rises out of the intricate and beautiful lace of seasoned relationships. Such things take time. Murray has stayed in it for the long haul and finds himself honored.

Finally, textbook theory and correct professional practice aside, Murray knows that philanthropy will only flourish as it should in this world when it captures the imagination of the man and woman on the street. As long as philanthropy is primarily perceived as the domain of the wealthy, it will fail to move people. Main Street still matters. The profession must have the common touch. Murray does.

Energy, calling, leadership, mentoring, creativity, persistence, anonymity, loyalty, the common touch—these are just some of the qualities through which Milton Murray has *given,* in the truest sense, to his profession and society. Together they comprise a remarkable gift—a gift worthy even of a great philanthropist.

References

Abingdon Press. *1990 Yearbook of American and Canadian Churches.* Nashville, Tenn.: Abingdon Press, 1990.

Abingdon Press. *1978 Yearbook of American and Canadian Churches.* Nashville, Tenn.: Abingdon Press, 1978.

Brakeley, G. A. *Tested Ways to Successful Fund Raising.* New York: American Management Association, COM Executive Books, 1980.

"Breaking the Ground." Emmanuel Missionary College (Andrews University). *Student Movement,* 1919, *4*(15), 1-2, 22.

Dickinson, E. "I'm Nobody! Who Are You?" In T. H. Johnson (ed.), *The Poems of Emily Dickinson.* Cambridge, Mass.: Harvard University Press, 1983.

Fisher, J. L. *Power of the Presidency.* New York: Macmillan, 1984.

Fisher, J. L., and Quehl, G. H. *The President and Fund Raising.* New York: Macmillan, 1989.

Forbes, Inc. *Thoughts on the Business of Life.* New York: Forbes, Inc., 1976.

Greenleaf, R. K. *Servant Leadership: A Journey into the Nature of Legitimate Power and Greatness.* New York: Paulist Press, 1977.

Greenleaf, R. K. *Teacher as Servant*. New York: Paulist Press, 1979.

Joseph, J. *The Charitable Impulse*. New York: Foundation Center, 1989.

Kouzes, J., and Posner, B. *The Leadership Challenge: How to Get Extraordinary Things Done in Organizations*. San Francisco: Jossey-Bass, 1987.

Lawson, D. *Give to Live*. La Jolla, Calif.: ALTI Publishing, 1991.

"New Music Building Forms $6000 Goal." Emmanuel Missionary College (Andrews University). *Student Movement*, 1919, *4*(14), 1.

Panas, J. *Born to Raise*. Chicago: Pluribus Press, 1988.

Seymour, H. J. *Campañas Para Obtención de Fondos*. Mexico City: Editorial Limusa-Wiley, 1970.

Seymour, H. J. *Designs for Fund-Raising*. (2nd ed.) Rockville, Md.: The Fund-Raising Institute, 1988.

Tippet, H. M. *Who Waits in Faith*. Washington, D.C.: Review and Herald Publishing Association, 1951.

Vande Vere, E. K. *The Wisdom Seekers*. Nashville, Tenn.: Southern Publishing Association, 1972.

Index